SOUTH-WEST S~   D

Other Chambers Scottish Guides

South-East Scotland
Kristina Woolnough

Highlands and Islands
Roger Smith

Chambers Scottish Guides

SOUTH-WEST SCOTLAND

Stuart Bathgate

Series editor
Kristina Woolnough

Chambers

Published 1992 by W & R Chambers Ltd
43–45 Annandale Street, Edinburgh EH7 4AZ

British Library Cataloguing in Publication Data

A catalogue record for this book is available from the British
Library

ISBN 0–550–22100–8

Acknowledgements
National and Regional Fact Files compiled by Donald Greig
Maps and town plans by Baynefield Carto-Graphics Ltd

Cover design by Creative Link, Edinburgh
Typeset by Hewer Text Composition Services, Edinburgh
Printed in England by Clays Ltd, St Ives, plc

CONTENTS

Chambers Scottish Guides

Scotland has traditionally been celebrated for two outstanding features: its history and its scenery. Romantic, compelling figures such as Robert the Bruce, Mary Queen of Scots and Bonnie Prince Charlie move across an historical landscape which is spiced with power-broking, love, political and religious intrigue, lust, murder and treachery.

Their names are known all over the world and the enduring appeal of their stories is given additional impetus by the tangible, remaining historical sites. Scattered throughout Scotland, from the Borders northwards, are battlefields where lands and crowns were won and lost and where uprisings succeeded and failed. There are caves, churches and castles where secular and religious courts were held and where refuge was sought. And there are palaces where kings and queens were born and died. As well as the buildings and ruins that document the fortunes of nobles and Scottish royalty, humbler stone monuments, settlements, houses and cottages can also be seen. These, from the prehistoric stone circles and standing stones to the 'black houses' of the Western Isles, represent largely unknown, unrecorded people who were either too ancient or too ordinary to capture the world's imagination.

Scotland's historical heritage is complemented by the country's natural heritage. The stock images of Scotland are invariably the photogenic Highland ones: jagged mountains, clear-eyed lochs and shaggy heath. Often overlooked are the more subtle charms of the Borders hills, or the hidden south-western corner of Scotland which lies around the Solway Firth. Mistakenly by-passed too is the sometimes dramatic, often picturesque east coast of the country, which stretches with indents of sandy crescents and fishing harbours from the Borders to Duncansby Head.

History, natural setting and human achievement marry in Scotland's towns and cities. Each place's architectural diversity, whether it involves loved and cherished buildings from the 17th, 18th and 19th centuries or the frequently controversial and sometimes hated efforts of the 20th century, fuses the past and the present.

For Scotland is not a museum, nor is it a national park, nor just a monument to past human endeavour. The fact of contemporary Scotland is a vital, intriguing one. New industries are slowly replacing old ones. A thriving contemporary urban culture –

theatre, fiction, popular music – is successfully blending with the traditional, predominantly Highland, culture of dancing, tartan, bagpipes, accordion bands and Gaelic ceilidhs. This blending exists at the large cultural annual fixtures like the Edinburgh Festival and Glasgow's Mayfest and it exists across Scotland at the plethora of smaller-scale, local celebrations which include music festivals, family fun-days and Highland shows.

The historical and the scenic, the traditional and the contemporary – *Chambers Scottish Guides* confirm all that is known and celebrated about Scotland and they also uncover the unknown, the less familiar and the forgotten corners. The guides will be an invaluable source of reference for visitors and for residents alike. Both can take advantage of the comprehensive Gazetteer of places and attractions, both can make use of the listings of theatres, cinemas, festivals, local media, nightlife, transport and galleries. Whether employed for suggestions for family outings, Sunday jaunts or for all-season holidays, *Chambers Scottish Guides* will inform, inspire and enlighten.

As well as providing the invaluable Gazetteer and listings, *Chambers Scottish Guides* offer a broad, sometime idiosyncratic, view of Scotland in the subject panels which are interspersed throughout the Gazetteer. These panels look at aspects of Scottish history, Scottish culture and contemporary Scottish life from football to conservation. From these panels, an impression emerges of a diverse, challenging, fascinating country, one that is inspired by its past and is also tripped up by it, and one that is struggling consciously and successfully for its future. If you think you know Scotland well, there is yet more to discover. If you are travelling in Scotland for the first time, these books will guide your journey.

How to use this book

Each *Chambers Scottish Guide* consists of three sections:

The **National Fact File**, which includes information on national Scottish organizations, sports associations, airports, mainline train stations, media, Scottish currency and accommodation.

The **Regional Fact File**, which contains listings of cinemas, theatres, media, festivals, public transport facilities, tourist information offices, airports, galleries and museums specifically for the area covered by each book.

The **Gazetteer**, which provides comprehensive A–Z information about cities, towns, villages, historical sites and visitor attractions within the regions covered by each book.

The **National Fact File** is arranged alphabetically by subject and then alphabetically by entry.

The **Regional Fact File** is ordered alphabetically by subject, then by town, city or village and then alphabetically by entry.

The **Gazetteer** is alphabetical and contains entries on cities, towns and villages, and visitor attractions within each guide's area. The Gazetteer also contains several special-feature panels, which look more closely at subjects, phenomena, people and historical events associated with the area. In addition, there are a number of maps and town plans. Gazetteer entries begin with the entry heading and then give an indication of location. Mileages given are for guidance only and are not strict road mileages. Addresses, opening hours, telephone numbers and an indication of disabled access follow where appropriate. 'Free' denotes no admission charge; an entrance fee should otherwise be assumed. The letters HS or NTS before the telephone number show that the property or land is owned or managed by Historic Scotland or the National Trust for Scotland. We have adopted the Scottish Tourist Board's definitions of disabled access, and it should be noted that in many cases the visitor attractions have defined their own accessibility. It is advisable for disabled visitors to check in advance. The symbols used are:

D – unassisted disabled access

D (P) – partial access

D (A) – access with assistance

Where no letter is given, it should be assumed that access has not been assessed in the STB's scheme or that access is difficult or impossible.

Comprehensive cross-references to other Gazetteer entries

and to panels have been included for ease of use. For example: **Football**, see panel p99. Other cross references from within one gazetteer or panel entry to another are highlighted by the use of **bold type**.

In the case of the major cities and towns – Aberdeen, Dundee, Edinburgh, Glasgow, Inverness, Perth and St Andrews, visitor attractions have been alphabetically entered as sub-headings under the main city or town heading. This procedure has also been adopted for islands and island groups.

It should be noted that three-figure telephone numbers are in the process of being phased out in Scotland. At the time of going to press, number changes had not all been implemented.

INTRODUCTION TO THE SOUTH-WEST

Strathclyde, Dumfries and Galloway, and Central are the regions covered by this book. While these boundaries are perhaps arbitrary, each of the three none the less has its own distinguishing characteristics.

The region of Strathclyde, with Glasgow at its heart, is home to approximately half of Scotland's five million people. While the bulk of the population is concentrated on Glasgow and its satellite industrial towns, the sprawling region also takes in Ayrshire (which includes Alloway, birthplace of Scotland's national poet Robert Burns), Loch Lomond, the best-known and most loved of Scotland's lochs, and the southern islands, from Bute and Arran in the Firth of Clyde to Mull, Iona, Coll and Tiree, part of the Inner Hebrides group.

Arran and Bute – in particular their respective capitals, Brodick and Rothesay – have long been popular holiday resorts or day-trip destinations for Scottish city-dwellers. The Hebrides, less accessible to day-trippers, still offer the opportunity to get away from it all. The one partial exception is Iona, where a settlement was established by St Columba in the sixth century; the current Iona community has been so successful in establishing the island as a place of religious retreat that, paradoxically, it can become quite crowded in summer.

The islands are reached by ferry – for example from Oban in the case of Mull, and from Ardrossan in the case of Arran. Ardrossan, in common with many other Clyde ports, is a holiday resort in its own right. Ayrshire coastal towns such as Troon and Girvan – and of course Ayr itself – offer good leisure facilities, with some of the best golf courses and beaches in Scotland.

The River Clyde is now chiefly devoted to leisure pursuits, but was once home of the world's greatest shipyards. It was shipbuilding, and other seafaring industries such as the tobacco trade with Virginia in the USA, that established Glasgow as Scotland's industrial centre. Now, like its river, Glasgow has been forced largely to abandon heavy industry in favour of the service economy. The process was not without its traumas, and even 15 years ago the predominant image of Glasgow was that of a depressed, socially deprived and violent city. The transformation in the ensuing years has been remarkable. Astute publicity campaigns by the district council, the Glasgow Garden Festival of 1988, and the year as European Capital of Culture in 1990 all transformed the image of Glasgow, until it is now rightly seen as one of the friendliest and liveliest cities in Britain.

Home to some remarkable Victorian buildings, and to works of genius such as architect Charles Rennie Mackintosh's School of

Art, Glasgow also boasts one of the finest municipal art collections in Britain. Located on the outer edge of the city is the Burrell Collection, the result of a life's work by the voraciously eclectic collector Sir William Burrell. Glasgow has pioneered city-centre regeneration, as typified by the Merchant City area, but has also – perhaps surprisingly for a place with a history of heavy industry – a remarkable number of green spaces, including public parks such as Glasgow Green and Kelvingrove; indeed, the name Glasgow means 'dear green place'.

A sharp contrast to Scotland's largest city, Dumfries and Galloway is a region of forests, farms and small market towns, extending from the Rhinns of Galloway in the far west to, at the eastern extreme, Langholm, which, with its rugby-playing heritage, seems to have more in common with Borders' traditions. The Solway Firth in the south is home to a rich variety of wildlife, while Whithorn, on the Solway coast, is believed to have been the birthplace of Christianity in Scotland. The south-eastern sector of the region borders England, and includes the famous settlement at Gretna, where under-age couples from the south would come to be married against the wishes of their families.

Dumfries and Galloway is relatively underdeveloped as a tourist destination, remaining quiet, relaxed and above all peaceful. Needless to say, the region has seen more warlike times and, until the Border with England was finally agreed upon, the area frequently witnessed skirmishes between marauding bands. But not all the conflict took place with the English. In the late Middle Ages the infamous reivers (or raiders) did not concern themselves with the nationality of the cattle they rustled.

Scotland's greatest monarch, Robert the Bruce, partly owed his crown to an act of violence. It was at Greyfriars Monastery in Dumfries that Bruce quarrelled with and killed his rival, John Comyn. With the internal opposition nullified, Bruce went on to free the country from the occupying English forces. It was in what is now Central Region that the decisive battle in the Wars of Independence was fought, at Bannockburn outside Stirling.

The position of Stirling and its castle was of pivotal importance in determining who controlled the country. To the north of the town lie the Highlands; from the castle ramparts, the view west stretches, weather permitting, towards Ben Lomond, Scotland's southernmost Munro (as all the mountains over 3000 feet are known); and, standing on the upper reaches of the River Forth, Stirling has always been within easy striking distance of the capital, Edinburgh.

Central Region today still straddles the land, and is just as diverse as its western neighbour Strathclyde, albeit on a smaller scale. At its easternmost end, on the Forth, close to Lothian Region,

lies industrial Grangemouth, with its oil refinery. To the east of
Stirling, the Hillfoots are a pleasant string of villages, such as Alva
and Tillicoultry, which were once dominated by mills and which
lie at the foot of the Ochil Hills. At the heart of Central Region
lie the Trossachs, one of the loveliest parts of Scotland, extending
roughly from Callander to the Queen Elizabeth National Forest
Park. Although extremely popular with tourists, who enjoy such
facilities as the watersports centre at Lochearnhead, the Trossachs
also contain areas of wilderness, accessible only on foot, which
are home to an abundance of wildlife. Also in the Trossachs is the
village of Balquhidder, stamping ground of the legendary outlaw Rob
Roy Macgregor and his family. Beyond the Trossachs, in the most
northerly section of Central (and stretching into Tayside Region),
lies Breadalbane, originally an estate owned by the earls of that name,
and still a remote, sparsely populated area. Killin to the east, and
Tyndrum and Crianlarich to the west, are its largest communities.

Both of the latter settlements are stopping points towards the
northern end of the West Highland Way, the long-distance footpath
which begins in Milngavie, on the outskirts of Glasgow. It is a
reminder that, even from the city, the remote parts of the Highlands
are not far away. The splendid diversity of south-west Scotland is all
the more remarkable in that it exists within such a compact area.

National Fact File

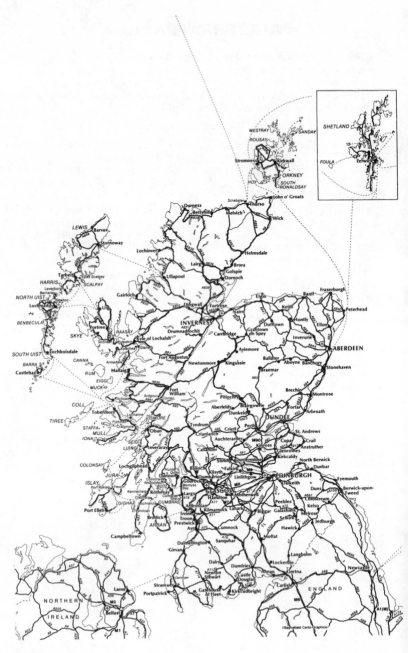

Scotland

ACCOMMODATION

The Scottish Tourist Board (STB: see under **Information – Associations and Organizations**) publishes a number of annual guides containing details of accommodation and grading systems throughout the country. A comprehensive booking service is offered by **Hi-Line**, run as part of the **Highland Direct Reservation System**.

CARAVANS AND CAMPING

A voluntary classification and grading scheme exists, run by the National Federation of Site Operators and the National Caravan Council, with the support of the Scottish Tourist Board (STB). Range of facilities is indicated on a descending scale from A to D, and quality of facilities by the number of ticks, varying 4–1. Other symbols are used to denote facilities, size and location of park, nature of park (static or touring), and standard of static caravans available for hire (also graded A–D). All parks in the scheme comply with the basic requirements of their site licence and, in general, with STB standards, and all have water and fire points and, where necessary, toilet blocks etc. In addition, a Thistle Commendation Scheme also indicates Holiday Static Caravan Parks, which let first-class caravans, combined with good facilities and an attractive environment. All commended parks which meet the requirements will display a Thistle plaque. Full details of sites involved in the scheme are available in STB's *Scotland: Camping and Caravan Parks*.

HOTELS, GUEST HOUSES AND SELF-CATERING

A voluntary classification and grading scheme is run by the STB, which sends inspectors to all hotels, guest houses, self-catering and bed and breakfast establishments wishing to be included. Gradings are awarded for quality, and classification indicates the range of services and facilities. Gradings are categorized as Approved (acceptable quality); Commended (good); Highly Commended (high), and Deluxe (excellent). Classification is signified by the number of crowns, varying 1–5 (minimum–comprehensive). Highly Commended Two Crown therefore indicates higher quality than Commended Four Crown, but offering fewer services and facilities. Full details of listed establishments are available in STB's *Scotland: Hotels and Guest Houses*, *Scotland: Bed and Breakfast* and *Scotland: Self-Catering Accommodation*.

YOUTH HOSTELS

There are 80 youth hostels in Scotland, categorized A–C in descending order, indicating facilities available. All offer dormitory accommodation and self-catering facilities. Full details are available from the Scottish Youth Hostels Association (see **Information – Associations and Organizations**), which publishes a handbook for youth hostellers in Scotland.

HIGHLAND DIRECT RESERVATION SYSTEM (HI-LINE)

Run by Highlands and Islands Enterprise, Highland Direct is an accommodation reservation service specifically for the Highlands and Islands. A brochure of all participating establishments is available by calling 0349 63434, while reservations (as well as travel information) can be made on 0349 65000 (see Highland Direct under **Information – Associations and Organizations**).

ACTIVITIES AND PASTIMES

The organizations listed here cover a range of sports and pastimes which may be of interest to the visitor. Anyone wishing to become involved with a certain activity during their stay in Scotland should contact the relevant organization. A complete list is available from the Scottish Sports Council (see **Information – Associations and Organizations**).

ARCHERY

Scottish Archery Association: Coaching Organizer, 4 Glowrorum Drive, Denny (0324 814380). Central body for archery in Scotland. Visitors may be invited to shoot with local clubs, 'as long as they hold FITA membership' (the international body for archery).

Scottish Field Archery Association: Don S. Smith, Secretary, 83 Woodend Road, Rutherglen, Glasgow (041–634 3108). Outdoor archery on a permanent woodland course of 28 targets.

ATHLETICS

Scottish Amateur Athletic Association/Scottish Women's Amateur Athletic Association: Secretary, Caledonia House, South Gyle, Edinburgh (031–317 7320/1).

BADMINTON

Scottish Badminton Union: Secretary, Cockburn Centre, 40 Bogmoor Place, Glasgow (041–445 1218).

BASKETBALL

Scottish Basketball Association: Secretary, Caledonia House, South Gyle, Edinburgh (031–317 7260).

BOWLING

Scottish Bowling Association: Secretary, 50 Wellington Street, Glasgow (041–221 8999).

Scottish Indoor Bowling Association: Secretary, 41 Montfode Court, Ardrossan, Ayrshire (0294 68372).

Scottish Women's Bowling Association: Secretary, 55A Esplanade, Greenock (0475 24140).

Scottish Women's Indoor Bowling Association: Secretary, 1 Underwood Road, Rutherglen, Glasgow (041–647 5810).

CAMPING

The Camping and Caravanning Club (Scottish Region): Ally Park, 56 Polwarth Avenue, Brightons, Falkirk (0324 715264). Scottish branch of the international affiliated organization for campers and caravanners.

CANOEING

Scottish Canoe Association: Secretary, Caledonia House, South Canoeing *cont* Gyle, Edinburgh (031–317 7314). Produces a number of videos and supplies, as well as a booklet listing names and addresses of clubs and coaching organizations throughout Scotland. Also produces a guide to

Scottish rivers, available from the above address.

CAVING

Grampian Speleological Group: 8 Scone Gardens, Edinburgh (031–661 1123).

CRICKET

Scottish Cricket Union: Secretary, Caledonia House, South Gyle, Edinburgh (031–317 7247. Produces a *Guide to Scottish Cricket* giving details of fixtures and results and including a Scottish directory of clubs, associations, universities and schools.

CURLING

Royal Caledonian Curling Club: Secretary, 2 Coates Crescent, Edinburgh (031–225 7083). A popular game among the Scots, curling is played on ice and involves sliding heavy stones with handles (curling stones) down a rink towards a target (tee).

CYCLING

CTC Scottish Cycling Council: Secretary, 11 Torridon Place, Kirkcaldy, Fife (0592 262944).

DANCE

Royal Scottish Country Dance Society: Secretary, 12 Coates Crescent, Edinburgh (031–225 3854). Worldwide society promoting Scottish Country Dance, organizing dances and events and offering instruction from beginner level to teaching standard.

Scottish Official Board of Highland Dancing: Secretary, Heritage House, 32 Grange Loan, Edinburgh (031–668 3965 a.m. only). World governing body for Highland Dancing offering information to visiting Highland dancers about championships, competitions and Highland Games they may wish to attend, and procedure for entering events.

DISABLED

Scottish Sports Association for the Disabled: Administrator, Fife Sports Institute, Viewfield Road, Glenrothes (0592 771700).

FISHING

Scottish Anglers National Association: Secretary, 5 Cramond Glebe Road, Edinburgh (031–312 7618). Governing body for the sport of game fishing in Scotland. The association does not provide an advice service to visitors, but does produce an annual report, available for a fee, which includes a useful 'Guide to SANA Club Waters', detailing clubs, waters, species, seasons and permit addresses.

Scottish Salmon Angling Federation: Secretary, 18 Abercromby Place, Edinburgh (031–556 4466).

FOOTBALL

Scottish Amateur Football Association: Secretary, Beechwood, Gateside Road, Barrhead, Glasgow (041–881 4025).

Scottish Football Association: 6 Park Gardens, Glasgow (041–332 6372). The sport's main governing body.

Scottish Football League: Secretary, 188 West Regent Street, Glasgow

(041–248 3844). Publishes the *Scottish Football League Review* giving details of all clubs, and contact names and addresses.

Scottish Women's Football Association: Administrator, Kelvin Hall, Argyle Street, Glasgow (041–337 1455).

GAMES
(HIGHLAND AND BORDER)

Scottish Games Association: Secretary, 24 Florence Place, Perth (0738 27782). Central organization for Highland and Border Games throughout Scotland.

GENEALOGY

Scottish Genealogy Society: 15 Victoria Terrace, Edinburgh (031–220 3677). Nominal membership fee. Does not carry out professional record searching, but can supply members with a list of professional researchers.

GLIDING

Scottish Gliding Association: Secretary, Glenfinart Park, Ardentinny, near Dunoon, Argyll (0369 81256).

GOLF

Scottish Golf Union: Secretary, The Cottage, 181A Whitehouse Road, Edinburgh (031–339 7546).

Scottish Ladies Golfing Association: Secretary, Chacewood, 49 Fullarton Drive, Troon (0292 313047).

HANG GLIDING

Scottish Hang Gliding Federation: Peter Shields, Secretary, 1 Lochbrae Drive, High Burnside, Glasgow (041–634 6688). Scotland has only one hang gliding school, Cairnwell Hang Gliding School, Cairnwell Mountain, by Braemar, Aberdeenshire (03397 41331). Visitors already qualified should contact the above address in Glasgow for information on the nearest club.

HOCKEY

Scottish Hockey Union: Executive Administrator, Caledonia House, South Gyle, Edinburgh (031–317 7254). Contact point for non-national clubs and associations interested in participating in Scotland.

ICE HOCKEY

Scottish Ice Hockey Association: President, 16 Glencairn Road, Ayr (0292 266203).

LACROSSE

Scottish Lacrosse Association: Secretary, Geddes House, Parleyhill, Culross, Dunfermline (0383 880602).

LAWN TENNIS

Scottish Lawn Tennis Association: Secretary/National Coach, 12 Melville Crescent, Edinburgh (031–225 1284).

LITERATURE

Association for Scottish Literary Studies: c/o Department of English Literature, University of Glasgow, Glasgow (041–339 8855 ext 5549). National association promoting the study, teaching and writing of

Scottish literature and the study and teaching of Scottish languages.

Poetry Association of Scotland: Secretary, 38 Dovecot Road, Edinburgh (031–334 5241). Originally established in 1924, the association is today a registered charity promoting poetry through readings and related activities.

MOUNTAINEERING

The Mountaineering Council of Scotland: Kevin Howett, National Officer, Flat 1R, 71 King Street, Crieff (0764 4962). Representative body for Scottish hill-walkers, rock and ice climbers, ski mountaineers and cross-country skiers of all standards. It directly funds winter and summer training courses for members at Glenmore Lodge in the Cairngorms (the national Scottish Outdoor Centre).

ORIENTEERING

Scottish Orienteering Association (SOA): Secretary, 7 Lawson Avenue, Banchory (033 02 3145). Formed in 1961, the association is now a subsidiary branch of the British Orienteering Federation (BOF), the governing body of the sport in the UK, which is affiliated to the International Orienteering Federation.

PARACHUTING

Scottish Sport Parachute Association: Secretary, 47 Great Southern Road, Aberdeen (0224 586510).

PARAGLIDING

Cloudbusters Paragliding School: Peter Shields, Chief Inspector,

9 Lynedoch Place, Glasgow (041–634 6688). Courses available for novices to advanced pilots. Information about nearest clubs available from the above address.

PÉTANQUE

Scottish Pétanque Association: Bob Boyle, National Secretary, 1 Arbroath Crescent, Stirling (0786 70619). The National Secretary of the association defined pétanque (peyt-onk) as being the 'proper name for the French game of boules'. With the exception of a few events which are only open to licensed players, all games are open to the public. Lists of affiliated clubs and contacts and a fixtures list are available from the above address.

RAMBLING AND RIGHTS OF WAY

The Ramblers' Association (Scotland): Scottish Officer, Kelinbank, Church Place, Freuchie, Fife (0337 58065).

Scottish Rights of Way Society: Secretary, Mrs Judith Lewis, John Cotton Business Centre, 10/2 Sunnyside, Edinburgh (031–652 2937).

RIDING

Scottish Trekking and Riding Association: Secretary, Tomnagairn Farm, Trochry, by Dunkeld (035 03 220).

ROWING

Scottish Amateur Rowing Association: Secretary,

11 Spottiswoode Street, Edinburgh (031–229 2366).

RUGBY

Scottish Rugby Union: Secretary, Murrayfield, Roseburn Street, Edinburgh (031–337 9551).

SHINTY

The Camanachd Association: Secretary, Algarve, Badabrie, Banavie, Fort William (0397 772461). A game like hockey, shinty is played mainly in the Highlands and Islands with a curved stick called a caman.

SHOOTING

British Association for Shooting and Conservation: Director of Development – Scotland, Scottish Centre, Trochry, by Dunkeld (035 03 226).

Scottish Clay Target Association: Secretary, 10 Balgibbon Drive, Callander (0877 31323).

SKIING

Scottish National Ski Council: Administrator, Caledonia House, South Gyle, Edinburgh (031–317 7280). Governing body representing and regulating skiing in Scotland. Produces a number of leaflets about its activities and skiing in Scotland.

SUB AQUA

Scottish Sub Aqua Club: Secretary, Cockburn Centre, 40 Bogmoor Place, Glasgow (041–425 1021). Central organization for sub aqua and diving clubs throughout Scotland.

SURFING

Scottish Surfing Federation: Secretary, South Pitblae House, Fraserburgh (0346 23600).

TUG-OF-WAR

Scottish Tug-of-War Association: Fiona Watson, Secretary, Laurelbank, 3 Riverside Villas, Catrine, Mauchline (0290 51502).

WATER SKIING

Scottish Water Ski Association: Secretary, Caledonia House, South Gyle, Edinburgh (031–317 7217).

WINDSURFING

Scottish Windsurfing Association: Secretary, c/o RYA Scotland, Caledonia House, South Gyle, Edinburgh (031–317 7217). The association publishes a guide to recognized windsurfing centres throughout the UK and abroad.

YACHTING

Royal Yachting Association Scotland: Secretary, Caledonia House, South Gyle, Edinburgh (031–317 7388). Videos, handbooks and log books for all RYA training and examination schemes are available from the above address. The *RYA Yearbook and Race Programme* is a useful guide to sailing in Scotland, giving comprehensive details of affiliated clubs and organizations, events and topics of general interest to all in the sailing community.

FESTIVALS (NATIONAL) AND PUBLIC HOLIDAYS

FESTIVALS

Burns Night: 25 January.
Celebrations marking the birthday of Scotland's national poet Robert Burns in 1759 have no effect on public facilities and services. Burns Night Suppers are held either on the evening of the 25th or on nearby dates at hotels, local halls, and in private houses.

St Andrew's Day: 30 November.
Celebrations for Scotland's patron saint do not constitute a statutory public holiday, and few amenities are affected. In the evening, St Andrew's Night dances and ceilidhs are held in hotels and local halls.

PUBLIC HOLIDAYS

English public holidays do not apply in Scotland, although some English-associated companies do recognize them. Bank holidays affect banks only. The following list gives the main bank holidays each year: 1 January*, 2 January, Friday before Easter, first and last Monday in May, first Monday in August, 30 November, 25 December*, 26 December. Spring and autumn holidays are taken instead of public holidays. Dates vary from year to year, but are usually on a Monday. Local holidays marking particular dates or occasions relevant to specific areas vary considerably between towns and regions. Full details of public holidays are available in *Public Holidays in Scotland*, published and updated annually by the Glasgow Chamber of Commerce (30 George Square, Glasgow (041–204 2121). The booklet costs £1.00. The STB publishes a free booklet, *Events in Scotland*, which lists events and festivals for the year throughout the country.

* New Year's Day and Christmas Day are taken by shops, offices, factories etc, although many hotels may remain open.

FOOD AND DRINK

DRINKING

Licensed hotels can serve drinks to residents at any time. Although licensing laws allow bars to open for 12 hours a day, public houses are usually open 1100–1430, and 1700–2300, Monday–Sunday, although not all choose to open on Sunday, and many, especially in cities, stay open later (some until 0130–0200). The same restrictions apply to licensed restaurants.

The legal age for drinking in Scotland is 18. Some landlords and publicans reserve the right to refuse admittance to minors, so it is always advisable to ask permission to bring children in.

Off-licences (liquor stores) selling beers, wines and spirits for private consumption are generally open 1100–2200 (Monday–Saturday, closed Sunday). It is illegal for anyone under the age of 18 to attempt to buy alcohol from an off-licence.

Scottish beer comes in a variety of forms. The standard request is for a pint of 'heavy' or 'special' but what exactly this means depends on what part of the country you're in. Generally, heavy is the equivalent of the Englishman's 'bitter', but is sweeter and fuller bodied. If you ask for a pint of heavy in Edinburgh, you're likely to be served '80 shilling' or, if you specifically request it, '70 shilling'. A few pubs also serve '90 shilling'. All three are cask-conditioned beers which have carbon dioxide pumped through them, making them creamy rather than fizzy. Their names – 70, 80 and 90 shilling – refer to the original

price of a keg of beer in days gone by. Ninety shilling has the greatest proof (alcoholic content) and 70 the least. Elsewhere, the same request for a pint of heavy is likely to secure a pint of Special. These are pressurized beers which are fizzy rather than creamy. Lager is another option, originally imported from Germany and Denmark, but now produced in Scotland. A pressurized beer, it is roughly equal in strength to 70 shilling, although some stronger lagers are available.

Chasers are a small measure of spirit (usually whisky), drunk simultaneously with a pint of beer. Whisky remains one of Scotland's favourite drinks and best-known exports. A nip and a dram are both equal to roughly one measure. Visitors should note, however, that measures in Scotland tend to be larger than those in England.

PUBLIC HOUSES

The Scottish pub is something of an institution. Although in larger towns restaurants are now widely available, in more rural areas they can be few and far between, in which case it is the pub which provides a focal point for eating. Pubs provide an excellent alternative for a cheap and filling lunch or dinner. Some pubs offer a 'Family Room', usually to one side of the main bar, where minors can eat either on their own or with their parents.

RESTAURANTS

A voluntary listing scheme for restaurants was introduced by the STB in 1973. Called 'The Taste of Scotland', it is now independently run, and covers restaurants, inns and coffee shops throughout Scotland which have applied for membership and paid the required fee. All applicants are visited by inspectors and, if up to standard, subsequently included in *The Taste of Scotland Guide*. Participants display the Taste of Scotland logo, a soup tureen encircled by the words 'The Taste of Scotland'. A list of all participating establishments is available from the Taste of Scotland office (see **Information – Associations and Organizations**). Restaurant guides, such as *Michelin* and the *Good Food Guide*, generally contain a Scottish section, albeit somewhat limited, and there are one or two specifically Scottish food guides.

LANGUAGE

ENGLISH

Spoken throughout Scotland, although variations in accent can often be difficult to understand.

SCOTS

Dialects vary from region to region. Visitors are most likely to hear 'broad' Scots around Glasgow and the Central Region. Geographically, in the Borders and from Dundee northwards, dialects change frequently.

GAELIC

Gaelic is still a living language in the Outer Hebrides (road signs on the Isle of Lewis are exclusively in Gaelic and bilingual in the rest of the region) and in pockets elsewhere, such as the Isle of Skye. Roughly 87 000 people in Scotland (about 2 per cent of the population) either speak, read or write Gaelic. The language is undergoing something of a renaissance at present, and it is estimated that over 3000 Scots are now learning Gaelic. Forecasts are that by 1993 broadcasting time for Gaelic television programmes will have trebled to 300 hours (see **Sabhal Mor Ostaig,** and **An Comunn Gaidhealach** under **Information – Associations and Organizations**).

MEDIA

The magazines and newspapers listed below are published in Scotland for a specifically Scottish market. British national papers often have Scottish sections or correspondents. Freesheets are free local newspapers distributed to each home in a particular area, often aimed at a certain district of a city or rural community. Some, along with regional newspapers, are listed in the Regional Fact File.

MAGAZINES

The List: 14 High Street, Edinburgh (031–558 1191). Contemporary magazine covering art, books, clubs, film, music, sport, television, theatre and travel, particularly in the Central Belt, covering Glasgow and Edinburgh. Published fortnightly (Thursday) and available from bookshops and newsagents.

Scots Magazine: Bank Street, Dundee (0382 23131). Scotland's oldest magazine was first published in 1739 in Edinburgh. In addition to articles of general Scottish interest, it has regular features on areas of Scotland and aspects of Scottish culture, and a classified section covering holidays, accommodation, books, shooting, fishing, livestock, and public notices. On sale on the last Friday of every month, it is available either by subscription or from newsagents and some bookshops.

Scottish Field: The Plaza Tower, The Plaza, East Kilbride (03552 46444). Up-market, glossy magazine offering the best of Scottish contemporary life. Articles cover people, lifestyles, fashion, culture, landscape, natural history and attractions, as well as history and heritage. Published monthly and available from newsagents.

Scottish Historical Review: Company of Scottish History Ltd, Aberdeen University Press, Farmers Hall, Aberdeen (0224 630724). Intellectual/academic magazine of essays on Scottish history, book reviews and lists of articles written about Scotland. Available by subscription only from the above address.

Scottish Home and Country: 42 Heriot Row, Edinburgh (031–225 1934). 'The Magazine of the Scottish Women's Rural Institutes' was founded in 1924. Published monthly, it offers features on crafts, fashion, gardening, books and cookery, all with a strong Scottish emphasis. Available on subscription in Scotland and abroad.

Scottish World: PO Box 1, Oban, Argyll (0631 62079). Covers all aspects of life in Scotland, such as clans, history and art; published quarterly and available on subscription or from newsagents.

What's On: 9a St Bernard's Crescent, Edinburgh (031–332 0471). Describing itself as 'the magazine for the Scottish leisure and tourism industry', *What's On* rivals *The List* as Scotland's equivalent of *Time Out*, providing details of events around Scotland. Covers exhibitions, theatre, film, music, food and drink; published monthly and available from newsagents.

DAILY NEWSPAPERS

Daily Record: Anderston Quay, Glasgow (041–248 7000).

Dundee Courier and Advertiser: 7 Bank St, Dundee (0382 23131).

The Herald: 195 Albion Street, Glasgow (041–552 6255). Formerly called the *Glasgow Herald*.

Press and Journal: PO Box 43, Lang Stracht, Mastrick, Aberdeen (0224 690222).

The Scotsman: 20 North Bridge, Edinburgh (031–225 2468).

SUNDAY NEWSPAPERS

Scotland on Sunday: 20 North Bridge, Edinburgh (031–225 2468).

Scottish Sunday Express: Park House, Park Circus Place, Glasgow (041–332 9600).

Sunday Mail: Anderston Quay, Glasgow (041–242 3403).

Sunday Post: Courier Place, Dundee (0382 22214); 144 Port Dundas Road, Glasgow (041–332 9933).

NATIONAL RADIO

(Regional channels listed under Regional Fact File)

BBC Radio Scotland: Broadcasting House, Queen Margaret Drive, Glasgow (041–330 2345); Broadcasting House, Queen Street, Edinburgh (031–225 3131). MW: 810 kHz/370m, VHF: 92.95 MHz.

BBC1–5: can be received throughout the country on the following frequencies, although quality of reception varies:
Radio 1 – MW: 1053 kHz/285m, 1089 kHz/275m
VHF: 97.7–99.6 MHz.

Radio 2 – VHF: 88–90.2 MHz.
Radio 3 – MW: 1215 kHz/247m.
VHF: 90–92.5 MHz.
Radio 4 – LW: 198 kHz/1515m.
VHF: 95.8, 94.9 MHz.
Radio 5 – MW: 693 kHz, 909 kHz.
In addition, BBC Radio Scotland is broadcast on MW: 810 kHz/370m, VHF: 92.95 MHz.

There is no national independent radio channel (in 1992); some independent regional channels (listed separately) are available.

TELEVISION

BBC Scotland: Broadcasting House, Queen Margaret Drive, Glasgow (041–330 2345); Broadcasting House, Queen Street, Edinburgh (031–225 3131). BBC1 and BBC2 are both received throughout the country, with some programme variations from England, including Scottish news bulletins.

British Sky Broadcasting: 6 Centaurs Business Park, Grant Way, Isleworth, Middx (071–782 3000). Broadcasts five channels to special receivers.

Channel 4 Television Company Ltd: 60 Charlotte Street, London (071-631 4444). Programmes received nationally throughout Britain.

Independent Television Association: Knighton House, 56 Mortimer Street, London (071–636 6866). Central organization for independent television stations. ITV programmes vary between regions: Scottish Television (STV), Borders Television and Grampian Television are listed in Regional Fact Files.

MONEY AND BANKS

BANKING

Scotland has four national banks.

Bank of Scotland plc: Head Office, The Mound, Edinburgh (031–442 7777). Fully independent.

The Royal Bank of Scotland plc: Head Office, 42 St Andrew Square, Edinburgh (031–556 8555). Fully independent.

Clydesdale Bank plc: Head Office, 30 St Vincent Place, Glasgow (041–223 2000). Part of National Australia Bank group.

TSB Scotland plc: Head Office, 120 George Street, Edinburgh (031–225 4555). Part of the TSB Group (head office in London).

All four banks have branches in the major Scottish cities, while both the Royal Bank of Scotland and the Bank of Scotland provide a comprehensive network of branches and autotellers throughout the country, which can be used by cardholders from other banks. Signs showing which cards can be used are displayed at autotellers.

CURRENCY

Scottish currency is the same value as English currency, although there are variations in the design of banknotes depending on the bank of issue. One pound notes are still legal tender in Scotland, along with the new one pound coins.

TRAVEL AND TRANSPORT

AIRPORTS

Scotland's main airports are at Glasgow and Edinburgh. Regional airports are located at Aberdeen and Prestwick, and there are a number of smaller airfields throughout the country (Dundee, Inverness and around the Highlands and Islands). Regional airports are listed in Regional Fact Files. Central address: **Scottish Airports Ltd**: St Andrews Drive, Glasgow Airport, Paisley, Renfrewshire (041–887 1111).

BUSES/COACHES

Scottish Citylink: St Andrew Square Bus Station, Edinburgh (031–557 5717); Victoria Coach Station, 164 Buckingham Palace Road, London (071–730 0202).

Caledonian Express/Stagecoach: Walnut Grove, Kinfauns, Perth (0738 33481).
Both run services from London and cities throughout England to Aberdeen, Dumfries, Dundee, Edinburgh, Fort William, Glasgow, Inverness, Lochalsh, Oban, Perth and Stirling. Stagecoach also run to Thurso.
Details of coach times and routes are available from the **Travel Centre**, Buchanan Street Bus Station, Glasgow (041–332 7133).

Scottish Postal Board: Royal Mail Public Relations Unit, West Port House, 102 West Port, Edinburgh EH3 9HS. Post enquiries only. Produces an annual *Scottish Postbus Guide*, giving full details of postbus services throughout Scotland.

DRIVING

Driving in Scotland is on the left-hand side. The road network throughout the country is generally good, with either motorway or dual carriageway links between Glasgow, Edinburgh and the north, including Stirling, Perth and Dundee.

Visitors should take extra care when driving on small country roads – many of which are single-track – particularly in the north of the country. In addition, during wintertime it is advisable to check on relief maps whether routes go over high roads, as snow can soon block them.

FERRIES

Comprehensive ferry services are run, particularly around the north of the country and to outlying islands.

Caledonian MacBrayne Ltd (popularly known as Cal Mac): The Ferry Terminal, Gourock (0475 33755).

Orkney Islands Shipping Company Ltd: 4 Ayre Road, Kirkwall, Orkney (0856 2044).

P&O European Ferries: Enterprise House, Channel View Road, Dover (0304 203388).

P&O Ferries Orkney and Shetland Services: P&O Ferries Terminal, Jamieson's Quay, Aberdeen (0224 589111).

Sealink British Ferries: Sea Terminal, Stranraer (0776 2262).

Shetland Islands Council: Grantfield, Lerwick, Shetland (0595 2024).

Western Ferries (Argyll) Ltd/Western

Ferries Clyde Ltd: 16 Woodside Crescent, Glasgow (041–332 9766).

TRAINS

InterCity trains connect Scotland with the rest of the UK. If taking a bicycle on trains, check in advance about availability of space, as reservations are compulsory on some services. Full details are available in the leaflet *ScotRail Welcomes Cyclists*.

Edinburgh Waverley Station: Waverley Bridge (031–556 2451).

Glasgow Central Station: Gordon Street (041–204 2844).

Glasgow Queen Street Station: (041–204 2844).

TRAVEL TICKETS

Reduced Price Tickets: Issued by British Rail, these can save money on most routes around the country. Ask for details of Standard, Cheap Day and Saver tickets, as well as Weekly, Monthly and 3-Monthly season tickets if your stay in Scotland is longer.

Travelpass: Issued by Highlands and Islands Enterprise, Travelpass allows 8 or 13 days' unlimited travel around the Highlands and Islands, including the Outer Hebrides, by bus, train and ferry. Passes also cover travel by train or bus (Scottish Citylink) from Glasgow, Edinburgh or Aberdeen to the Highlands and back again. Further details, and passes, are available from British Rail in Edinburgh, Glasgow, Paisley, Aberdeen, Stirling and Inverness; from St Andrew Bus Station (Edinburgh), Buchanan Street Bus Station (Glasgow); and from Caledonian MacBrayne (address under Ferries above).

Festival Cities Rover: Issued by British Rail, this allows unlimited travel for any three or seven consecutive days between Edinburgh, Kirkcaldy, North Berwick, Stirling, Glasgow and intermediate stations.

Freedom of Scotland Rover Ticket: Issued by British Rail, this allows unlimited train travel (also covering Caledonian MacBrayne ferries and Firth of Clyde steamers) from Wick and Thurso in the north to Carlisle and Berwick in the south, for 4, 7, 10 or 15 days.

Highland Rover Airpass: British Airways offers a 'Highland Rover Airpass', which allows travel on up to eight Highlands and Islands flights over a minimum of eight days.

WEATHER

Misconceptions about Scottish weather are common: that the whole of
Scotland is covered by snow in winter for example, and that it rains a lot in
summer.

In fact the eastern part of Scotland is rather dry; the annual average
rainfall for Edinburgh is similar to that for London. The higher areas are
wet, but even there the rainfall is seasonal. In the west of Scotland the
driest months are April, May and June and the wettest are September to
January.

As for sunshine, the chart shows the extreme east of Scotland (Dunbar)
to have an excellent sunshine record (although the absolute record for
hours of sunshine in a day is held by Tiree with 329 hours in a month in
May 1946 and May 1975).

Full details of Scotland's climate are available in *The Climate of Scotland
– Some Facts and Figures*, on sale at HMSO Bookshops or from the
Meteorological Office, Saughton House, Broomhouse Drive, Edinburgh
(031–244 8362/3).

Average number of days with snow on ground at 9am (1951–80)

Location	Jan	Feb	Mar	Apr	May	Jun	Jul	Aug	Sep	Oct	Nov	Dec	Year
Shetland													
Lerwick	7.5	7.8	3.8	1.4	0.1	0.0	0.0	0.0	0.0	0.2	2.4	4.9	23.1
Western Isles													
Stornoway	3.5	2.8	1.4	0.2	0.0	0.0	0.0	0.0	0.0	0.0	1.0	1.5	10.4
Highland													
Wick	5.4	5.6	2.2	0.5	0.0	0.0	0.0	0.0	0.0	0.0	1.5	3.0	18.2
Nairn	5.5	5.6	1.7	0.2	0.0	0.0	0.0	0.0	0.0	0.0	0.8	2.7	16.5
Grampian													
Braemar	15.6	15.9	9.7	2.4	0.1	0.0	0.0	0.0	0.0	0.3	4.6	10.4	59.0
Craibstone (nr Aberdeen)	9.6	9.6	4.9	0.9	0.1	0.0	0.0	0.0	0.0	0.2	2.6	4.7	32.6
Tayside													
Perth	5.7	5.2	1.2	0.1	0.0	0.0	0.0	0.0	0.0	0.0	0.5	2.4	15.1
Lothian													
Edinburgh													
Royal Botanic Gdn.	5.0	5.3	1.1	0.2	0.0	0.0	0.0	0.0	0.0	0.0	0.5	1.9	14.0
Royal Observatory	5.5	6.1	1.8	0.3	0.0	0.0	0.0	0.0	0.0	0.0	1.0	2.0	16.7
Penicuik	9.6	9.3	3.8	0.9	0.1	0.0	0.0	0.0	0.0	0.0*	1.9	4.7	30.3
Dunbar	1.7	2.6	0.4	0.1	0.0	0.0	0.0	0.0	0.0	0.0	0.2	0.6	5.6
Strathclyde													
Tiree	1.4	1.2	0.4	0.1	0.0	0.0	0.0	0.0	0.0	0.0	0.1	0.4	3.6
Glasgow Airport	3.5	1.8	0.7	0.1	0.0	0.0	0.0	0.0	0.0	0.0	0.6	1.3	8.0
Auchincruive (nr Ayr)	2.3	1.7	0.7	0.1	0.0	0.0	0.0	0.0	0.0	0.0	0.5	0.6	5.9
Dumfries & Galloway													
Eskdalemuir	10.1	9.6	4.7	0.7	0.0*	0.0	0.0	0.0	0.0	0.0*	1.9	5.0	32.0

Note: 0.0* in the 30-year period indicates there was only one day with
snow lying at 0900 hours in this month.

Average rainfall in mm (1951–80)

Location	Jan	Feb	Mar	Apr	May	Jun	Jul	Aug	Sep	Oct	Nov	Dec	Year
Shetland													
Lerwick	127	93	93	72	64	64	67	78	113	119	140	147	1177
Orkney													
Kirkwall	105	71	72	54	53	57	55	77	88	110	120	121	983
Western Isles													
Benbecula	129	86	89	62	65	76	83	83	119	139	140	132	1203
Stornoway	115	77	80	66	62	67	72	74	103	126	129	125	1096
Highland													
Ullapool	119	84	93	76	73	83	80	92	115	155	159	161	1290
Achmore (nr Plockton)	104	68	70	56	56	63	78	82	107	112	124	112	1032
Portree (Skye)	182	116	129	93	91	104	113	118	170	204	203	210	1732
Onich (nr Fort William)	200	132	152	111	103	124	137	150	199	215	220	238	1981
Wick	81	58	55	45	47	49	61	74	68	73	90	82	783
Fort Augustus	112	72	83	58	72	61	65	82	103	124	126	140	1098
Nairn	48	34	33	36	43	46	62	75	50	54	60	52	593
Glenmore Lodge	96	64	71	68	76	73	87	107	80	96	100	106	1024
Grampian													
Gordon Castle	55	44	42	42	51	55	77	89	57	66	75	67	720
Braemar	93	59	59	51	65	55	58	76	73	87	87	96	859
Craibstone (nr Aberdeen)	77	57	54	51	62	54	79	83	68	78	80	80	821
Tayside													
Pitlochry	94	59	52	47	64	62	65	72	70	76	69	94	824
Arbroath	50	40	40	38	48	44	62	67	50	52	54	54	599
Perth	70	52	47	43	57	51	67	72	63	65	69	82	738
Fife													
St. Andrews	62	48	44	39	50	44	61	68	55	55	63	64	653
Lothian													
Edinburgh (Royal Botanic Garden)	47	39	39	38	49	45	69	73	57	56	58	56	626
Dunbar	46	33	33	33	47	41	55	68	47	48	55	49	555
Borders													
Floors Castle (Kelso)	55	43	38	40	55	51	63	75	57	59	63	57	656
Central													
Callander	164	113	115	81	97	86	97	113	141	147	175	193	1522
Strathclyde													
Tiree	120	71	77	60	56	66	79	83	123	125	123	123	1106
Inveraray Castle	210	132	150	115	106	124	137	148	209	225	228	252	2036
Eallabus (Islay)	139	85	92	70	67	74	93	93	128	139	149	149	1278
Glasgow Airport	96	63	65	50	62	58	68	83	95	98	105	108	951
Auchincruive (nr Ayr)	82	50	53	47	51	58	80	91	100	97	99	93	901
Aros (Mull)	210	116	142	97	96	109	120	133	199	208	203	220	1853
Dumfries & Galloway													
West Freugh (nr Stranraer)	100	65	67	53	55	57	70	82	98	100	105	103	955
Loch Dee	236	154	168	130	121	122	142	184	214	222	241	263	2197
Dumfries	103	72	68	55	71	63	77	93	104	106	109	104	1023
Eskdalemuir	150	99	108	86	94	95	107	122	142	140	153	160	1456

1″ = 25.4mm

Average bright sunshine in hours (1951–80)

Location	Jan	Feb	Mar	Apr	May	Jun	Jul	Aug	Sep	Oct	Nov	Dec	Annual	Annual total
Shetland														
Lerwick	0.7	1.9	2.7	4.5	4.9	5.3	4.0	3.8	3.2	2.0	1.1	0.5	2.9	1056
Orkney														
Kirkwall	1.0	2.3	3.1	4.9	5.2	5.4	4.3	4.1	3.4	2.4	1.3	0.7	3.2	1160
Western Isles														
Stornoway	1.2	2.5	3.6	5.2	6.0	5.9	4.2	4.4	3.6	2.5	1.5	0.8	3.4	1256
Benbecula	1.3	2.5	3.7	5.8	6.5	6.5	4.6	4.9	3.8	2.5	1.6	0.9	3.7	1361
Highland														
Prabost (Skye)	1.3	2.7	3.5	5.2	6.0	5.8	4.1	4.3	3.3	2.3	1.5	1.0	3.4	1243
Onich (nr Fort William)	0.9	2.2	2.9	4.4	5.3	5.0	3.7	3.8	2.9	2.1	1.1	0.6	2.9	1059
Wick	1.3	2.6	3.4	5.0	5.2	5.4	4.4	4.3	3.7	2.8	1.6	1.0	3.4	1240
Nairn	1.4	2.8	3.6	4.9	5.3	5.6	4.7	4.3	3.9	2.9	1.8	1.2	3.5	1290
Fort Augustus	0.8	2.1	2.9	4.2	5.0	5.0	3.8	3.8	2.9	2.0	1.0	0.6	2.9	1044
Glenmore Lodge (nr Aviemore)	0.8	2.4	3.4	4.4	5.1	5.2	4.2	4.1	3.5	2.6	1.1	0.5	3.1	1137
Grampian														
Braemar	0.8	2.0	2.9	4.5	5.2	5.5	4.9	4.2	3.4	2.1	1.1	0.6	3.1	1137
Craibstone (nr Aberdeen)	1.7	2.7	3.4	5.0	5.6	6.0	5.2	4.7	3.9	3.1	2.1	1.5	3.7	1367
Tayside														
Perth	1.4	2.3	3.2	5.1	5.7	6.0	5.5	4.5	3.7	2.7	1.8	1.1	3.6	1309
Arbroath	1.8	2.9	3.6	5.6	6.1	6.4	5.9	5.2	4.4	3.2	2.4	1.6	4.1	1499
Fife														
St. Andrews	1.8	2.6	3.4	5.1	5.8	6.2	5.6	4.9	4.2	3.1	2.2	1.5	3.9	1415
Lothian														
Edinburgh (Royal Botanic Garden)	1.5	2.4	3.2	4.9	5.7	6.1	5.5	4.8	4.0	3.0	2.0	1.3	3.7	1400
Dunbar	1.8	2.8	3.7	5.4	6.1	6.7	6.1	5.4	4.4	3.4	2.4	1.7	4.2	1523
Strathclyde														
Tiree	1.4	2.4	3.7	5.8	6.9	6.6	5.1	5.2	3.9	2.5	1.5	0.9	3.8	1400
Glasgow Airport	1.3	2.2	3.1	5.1	6.0	6.2	5.3	4.7	3.7	2.6	1.6	1.0	3.6	1303
Prestwick Airport	1.6	2.8	3.5	5.6	6.8	6.7	5.7	5.2	4.0	2.9	1.9	1.3	4.0	1465
Dumfries & Galloway														
Dumfries	1.5	2.5	3.2	4.9	5.8	6.1	5.1	4.9	3.7	2.9	2.0	1.3	3.7	1338
Eskdalemuir	1.3	2.2	2.9	4.5	5.3	5.4	4.6	4.3	3.3	2.5	1.8	1.2	3.3	1198

MISCELLANEOUS

EMERGENCY PHONE NUMBERS

Directory Enquiries: 192. Free
from phone-boxes; 42 pence per call
otherwise.

Operator: 100. Free.

**Police/Fire/Ambulance/Mountain
Rescue/Coastguard**: 999. Free.

LAW

The Scottish legal system differs
from that in England. Unlike most
legal systems, it is based neither
solely on Roman Law (as in France
and Germany), nor is it derived
completely from English law (as in
America). Instead, it is a mixture of
composite sources, having evolved
its principles over the centuries on
the basis of past cases.

The most senior lawyer in
Scotland is the Lord Advocate,
who is responsible for all criminal
prosecutions, discharging his
functions through the Crown
Office. He is also a member of the
government, although his role as a
lawyer takes precedence over that as
a politician.

The legal profession in Scotland
has two branches: advocates and
solicitors. Further information is
available from the **Law Society of
Scotland** (see under **Information –
Associations and Organizations**).

LOCAL GOVERNMENT

Scottish local government as it is
recognized today came into
existence on 16 May 1975. It is on

a two-tier basis, with nine regional
councils (such as Strathclyde,
Tayside and the Borders) and 53
district councils (such as Glasgow
City, Angus and Berwickshire).
In addition there are three island
councils for Orkney, Shetland and
the Western Isles which perform
the tasks of both regional and
district councils. In general, regional
councils provide large-scale services
such as transport and education
within their area, while district
councils are responsible for local
planning, housing, environmental
affairs, tourism and amenity
services.

POPULATION

Britain: 55 780 000 (1981).

Scotland: 5 130 735 (1981).

At the time of going to press,
preliminary figures of the 1991
census put Scotland's population at
4 957 289. Also apparent is the first
evidence of the 'urban clearances'
which have pushed up house prices
in many rural areas of the country,
with increasing numbers of people
leaving their homes in the city for
a peaceful retreat in the country.
It is estimated that over the past
two years (1989–91), almost 14 000
people have migrated to Scotland,
many from England. Islands such
as Skye, Mull and Arran now have
sizeable English populations.

RELIGION*

Of Scotland's various Christian
denominations, the largest is

the Church of Scotland, with an official membership of 822 985 (1988), although it is likely that considerably more people identify themselves as belonging to the Church of Scotland without formally being members of it. Its structure is presbyterian, with regions split into parishes, and its doctrine evangelical. It is governed by the General Assembly of the Church of Scotland, which meets once a year in Edinburgh in May to review policies and discuss reports. The Roman Catholic Church is Scotland's second largest, with 793 620 members (1988), while Scottish Episcopal Church membership stands at 59 940 (1987).

Also functioning along the lines of the presbyterian tradition is a conservative presbyterian group, with a membership of around 12 250 (1988). This includes the Reformed Presbyterian Church, found mostly in the Lowlands, and the Free Church of Scotland and Free Presbyterian Church, which are found mostly in the western Highlands and Islands.

Other religious groups present in Scotland include the Religious Society of Friends (Quakers), whose membership is around 550 (1988), and a number of Christian organizations, including Independent Evangelical Churches, various house Churches and the Christian Brethren, which have a combined total membership of over 17 800 (1984). Judaism

is represented, with Hebrew congregations in each of Scotland's four major cities accounting for 4200 people, while the Muslim population, mostly Asian, is estimated to be between 15 000 and 20 000 (1988). Hindus and Sikhs are also present (although no figures are available), and for several years now there has been a Buddhist community at Langholm in the Borders.

TELEPHONES

British Telecom pay-phones can be found throughout the country. Although the Mercury network is increasing, Mercury telephones are still found mostly in larger cities. British Telecom telephones accept either coins (all except one penny and the new five pence coins) or phone-cards; the latter are available from post offices and some newsagents. British Telecom has replaced the traditional red call-box (telephone booth) with modern glass booths, although a handful of old ones have been allowed to remain in locations where they have been thought more appropriate. New booths marked with a green stripe or sign accept phone-cards and those with a pink stripe or sign, coins. International Direct Dialling is possible to most countries.

TOURISM IN SCOTLAND

Tourism in Scotland has traditionally consisted of a three-month summer influx of visitors from June to August, followed by increased activity (both domestic and international) at the end and beginning of the year for the skiing season. Attributes constantly

* Statistics throughout are based on the Fact Sheet *Religion in Scotland*, issued by the Scottish Office (see Information – Associations and Organizations), in conjunction with HMSO. At the time of going to press a new Fact Sheet is being prepared, updated to provide comprehensive information on religion in Scotland, and available from the Scottish Office.

highlighted have been beautiful scenery, wild open spaces, the Edinburgh Festival in August, and the opportunity to indulge in some healthy country living.

This situation is changing, however, and the emphasis is no longer on making the most of a few months of the year, but on how to sustain tourism in Scotland right through from January to December, and in a way that brings maximum benefits to visitors and locals alike. As in so many countries around the world, Scotland is now trying to make the most of her resources without allowing them to become worn, run-down and over-exploited. To this end, moves are afoot throughout the country to implement new policies aimed at opening up less visited areas, raising standards of accommodation, and, generally, spreading the load more evenly in terms of both geographical location of attractions and seasonal accessibility. In addition, conservation bodies are continually working with all aspects of Scottish wildlife, fauna and flora (see **Information – Associations and Organizations** for a number of the main ones). For the visitor this will ensure a better quality of stay at any time of the year, while for the Scots it means the continued preservation of their land, and the ensuing economic benefits.

INFORMATION – ASSOCIATIONS AND ORGANIZATIONS

An Comunn Gaidhealach: 109 Church Street, Inverness (0463 231226). One of several Gaelic organizations based at the Church Street office, dealing with the Gaelic language and culture past and present.

Forestry Commission:
231 Corstorphine Road, Edinburgh (031–334 0303). A government department, the Forestry Commission manages over one million hectares of forest (60 per cent in Scotland), provides a source of employment and revenue in more rural areas, is responsible for training and research, and provides many recreational facilities.

Friends of the Earth Scotland: Bonnington Mill,
70–2 Newhaven Road, Edinburgh (031–554 9977). Scottish headquarters of environmental group.

Highlands and Islands Enterprise: Bridge House, 20 Bridge Street, Inverness (0463 234171). Development agency for the Highlands and Islands, investing roughly 25 per cent of its budget in tourism.

Highland Direct: Hi-Line House, Station Road, Dingwall, Ross-shire (0349 65000). A comprehensive holiday booking service run by Highlands and Islands Enterprise.

Historic Scotland: 20 Brandon Street, Edinburgh (opening times and admission charges, 031–244 3101; Friends of Historic Scotland, 031–244 3099; all other enquiries, 031–244 3144). Government body working to protect Scotland's

built heritage, caring for over 330 properties throughout Scotland, including Edinburgh and Stirling Castles, Dryburgh Abbey, the Meigle Sculptured Stones, Dallas Dhu Distillery and St Andrews Cathedral. Membership of 'Friends of Historic Scotland' is open to anyone and benefits include 'unlimited free entry (and directory) to all properties; concessions at English and Welsh monuments, and a quarterly newsletter'. For non-members Scottish Explorer Tickets are available for 7 or 14 days (family tickets also), offering reduced entrance fees to over 70 sites.

Law Society of Scotland:
26 Drumsheugh Gardens, Edinburgh (031–226 7411). The governing body of the solicitor branch of the Scottish legal profession.

National Trust for Scotland:
5 Charlotte Square, Edinburgh (031–226 5922). There are over 100 historic castles, houses, gardens and areas of open countryside in the Trust's care in Scotland. A registered charity, the National Trust for Scotland was formed in 1931 and now welcomes in excess of one and a half million people per year to properties in its care. Members are admitted free to all properties, while non-members are charged an entrance fee at most sites.

Royal Highland and Agricultural Society of Scotland: Edinburgh Exhibition and Trade Centre, Ingliston, Edinburgh (031–333 2444).

Royal Society for the Protection of Birds (Scotland): Scottish

Headquarters, 17 Regent Terrace, Edinburgh (031–557 3136). Scottish branch of the national organization, working to protect birds throughout Scotland. Produces a series of useful leaflets, as well as an excellent map, *Where to Watch Birds in Scotland*, matching areas of the country with species of birds.

Sabhal Mor Ostaig Gaelic School: An Teanga, Isle of Skye (04714 373). Started in 1973 as a summer school, Sabhal Mor Ostaig (The Big Barn) has grown to become a popular centre for innovative further education, as well as one of the world's leading authorities on Gaelic language and culture. Courses and information are offered on every aspect of Gaelic culture, from song and clarsach to language and writing skills.

Saltire Society: 9 Fountain Close, 22 High St, Edinburgh (031–556 1836). Promotes culture and heritage of Scotland through lectures, publications etc.

Scotland's Gardens Scheme: 31 Castle Terrace, Edinburgh (031–229 1870). Works with and publishes details of several hundred private gardens around Scotland which are periodically opened to the public. Directory available from the above address, or from outlets such as National Trust shops and Tourist Information Offices.

Scottish Arts Council: 12 Manor Place, Edinburgh (031–226 6051). Part of the Arts Council of Great Britain, promoting the arts in Scotland. Information on theatres throughout the country.

Scottish Conservation Projects: Balallan House, 24 Allan Park, Stirling (0786 79697). Conservation charity founded in 1984, inviting people of all ages to become involved in preserving the Scottish countryside. Working 'holidays' learning skills such as dry-stone dyking and wildlife management.

Scottish Enterprise: 120 Bothwell Street, Glasgow (041–248 2700). A Government-funded body which oversees and monitors development throughout the country. Grants aid towards development and administers the Enterprise Trust scheme.

Scottish Field Studies Association: Kindrogan Field Centre, Enochdhu, Blairgowrie, Perthshire (0250 81286). Offers courses at its Perthshire field centre aimed at increasing understanding of the Scottish countryside.

Scottish Natural Heritage: Battleby, Redgorton, Perth (0738 27921) and 12 Hope Terrace, Edinburgh (031–447 4784). In existence from 1 April 1992, created by the merger of the Countryside Commission for Scotland and the Nature Conservancy Council in Scotland. Functions include giving planning advice to authorities, providing financial assistance for tree-planting, landscape enhancement and recreation provisions establishing nature reserves, researching species and sites and granting aid to conservation bodies.

Scottish Office: Information Department, New St Andrew's House, Edinburgh (031–244 5199). The publicity office of Scotland's administrative headquarters produces a number of useful fact sheets about issues relevant to Scottish life today. These cover a wide range of topics, including religion, education and social work and are available by post or phone-call from the above address. No personal callers.

Scottish Sports Council: Caledonia House, South Gyle, Edinburgh (031–317 7200). Umbrella organization for sports in Scotland, information on main sporting bodies throughout the country.

Scottish Tartans Society: Scottish Tartan Museum, Drummond Street, Comrie, Perthshire (0764 70779). International headquarters maintaining the Register of all Publicly Known Tartans. Research department will answer questions 'on the origin of Scottish names, their connections with clans and families, and their associated tartans'. Fees are charged for time spent searching records and compiling reports. The society does not deal with enquiries concerning heraldry or genealogy. Individual and associate membership available.

Scottish Tourist Board: 23 Ravelston Terrace, Edinburgh (031–332 2433); 19 Cockspur Street, London (071–930 8661).

Scottish Wildlife Trust: 25 Johnston Terrace, Edinburgh (031–226 4602). Voluntary body conserving Scottish wildlife, with over 60 reserves throughout the country.

Scottish Youth Hostels Association: 7 Glebe Crescent, Stirling (0786 51191). Central office and information point for Scotland's 81 youth hostels.

Taste of Scotland: 33 Melville Street, Edinburgh (031–220 1900). (See listings under **Food and drink – Restaurants**.)

Regional Fact File

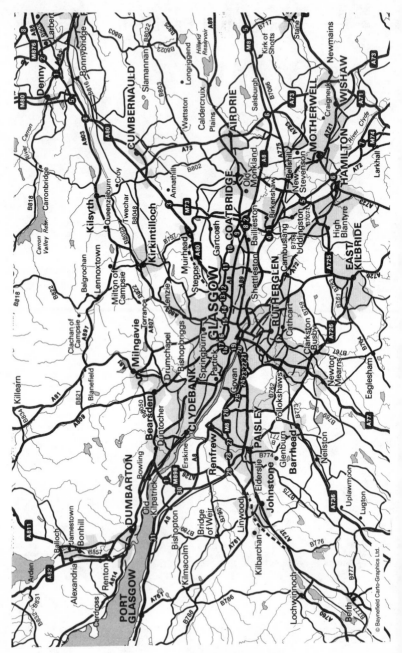

CINEMAS

Annan

Lady Street Cinema: Lady Street
(04612 202796).

Ayr

Odeon: Burns Statue Square
(0292 264049).

Bute, Isle of

Winter Garden: Victoria Street,
Rothesay (0700 502487).

Campbeltown

Picture House: 26 Hall Street
(0586 553657).

Castle Douglas

Palace Cinema: St Andrews Street
(0556 2141).

Clydebank

UCI Clydebank: 23 Britannia Way,
Clydebank Shopping Centre
(041–951 2022).

Dumfries

Cannon: Shakespeare Street
(0387 53578).

Robert Burns Centre Film Theatre: Mill
Road (0387 64808).

Dunoon

Studio Cinema: 41 John Street
(0369 4545).

East Kilbride

UCI: The 9 Cinemas, Olympia
Arcade (03552 49699/49622).

Falkirk

Cannon Cinema: Princes Street
(0324 31713).

Glasgow

Cannon Film Centre: Sauchiehall
Street (041–332 9513).

Cannon Cinemas: The Forge,
Parkhead (041–556 4282).

Cannon Muirend: Clarkston Road
(041–637 2641).

Glasgow Film Theatre: 12 Rose Street
(041–332 6535).

Hillhead Grosvenor Cinema: Ashton
Lane, off Byres Road (041–339 4298).

Hillhead Salon Cinema: Vinicombe
Street, off Byres Road
(041–339 4256).

Odeon: Renfield Street
(041–332 8701).

Gretna

Prize Cinema: Central Avenue
(0461 37591).

Hamilton

Odeon: Townhead Street
(0698 283802).

Kilmarnock

Cannon: Titchfield Street
(0563 25234)

Lockerbie

Rex Cinema and Bingo Club: Bridge
Street (057 62 2547).

Motherwell

Motherwell Moviehouse: Motherwell
Theatre (0698 67515).

Cinemas (cont.)

Newton Stewart

The Cinema: 35 Victoria Street
(0671 2058).

Oban

Highland Theatre: George Street
(0631 62444).

Paisley

Kelburne Cinema: Glasgow Road,
Paisley (041–889 3612).

Saltcoats

Kemp Cinemas: Hamilton Street
(0294 68999).

Stirling

Allan Park Cinema: Allan Park
(0786 74137).

Wishaw

Classic Cinema: 59 Kirk Road
(0698 372598).

FESTIVALS/EVENTS

The festivals listed below are those which are likely to be of most interest to visitors. Dates should be checked with Tourist Information Offices.

Alva
June–August: Thursday – Scottish Country Dance Season.
Mid July: Highland Games.

Annan
End May: South-West Athletics Championships.
July: Riding of the Marches (Common Riding).

Arran, Isle of
June, first and second week: Arran Festival of Folk.
Mid July: Lamlash Gala Week.
August, second week: Brodick Highland Games.

Ayr
May, first week: West of Scotland Agricultural Show.
June, first/second week: Ayrshire Arts and Robert Burns Festival.
Ayr Golf Week.

Balloch
Mid July: Highland Games.

Biggar
June, second/third week: Gala Week.
August, second week: Blackwood Murray Rally.
October: Clydesdale Arts Festival.
December 31: Ne'er Day Bonfire.

Blantyre
June, first week: Highland Games.

Bothwell
End August: Annual Flower Show.

Bridgend
August, second week: Agricultural Show.

Bridge of Allan
August, first week: Strathallan Highland Games and Pipe Band Championships.

Bute, Isle of
Early May bank holiday: Bute Jazz Festival.
August, first/second week: Agricultural Show.
Mid/end August: Highland Games.

Callander
August, first week: International Highland Games.

Campbeltown
Mid/end February: Kintyre District Drama Festival.
Mid June: Highland Games, part of Campbeltown Festival Week.
Mid/end June: Kintyre Music Festival.
End July/August: Agricultural Games.

Carmunnock
June: Highland Games.

Castle Douglas
August, first week: Stewartry Agricultural Show.
August, first/second week: Scottish Orienteering Championships; also in other places around the region.
August, third week: Dumfries and Galloway Horse Show.

Clackmannan
End May/June: Clackmannan District Festival.

Drymen
May: Agricultural Show.
September, first/second week:

Festivals/Events (cont.)

Flower, Vegetable and Handicraft Show.

Dumbarton

May: Agricultural Show.
Mid July: Dumbarton District Festival.

Dumfries

March/April: Easter Egg Hunt.
May/June: Dumfries and Galloway Arts Festival.
June, second/third week: Guid Nychburris Festival.
June, third/fourth week: Dumfries Book Fair.
End June: Dumfries Half Marathon.
August, first week: Dumfries and Lockerbie Agricultural Show.
August, second week: Forest Jazz Festival.
End September: Burns Festival.
End November (30): St Andrew's Day Firework Display.

Dunoon

End August: Cowal Highland Gathering.

East Kilbride

April–September: East Kilbride Outdoor Recreation Summer Season.
May, second and third weeks: Annual Sports Festival.
End May–June: Arts Festival.

Ecclefechan

August, first week: Burnswark Race.

Gatehouse of Fleet

End July/August: Gala Week.

Girvan

May, first week: Girvan Folk Festival.
End September: Girvan Jazz Festival.

Glasgow

May: Mayfest.

June: Lord Provost's Procession.
Glasgow Horse Show and Country Fair.
Royal Scottish Orchestra Promenade Concerts.
July: Glasgow Fair Summer Festival, Glasgow Green.
International Jazz Festival.
International Folk Festival.
August: World Pipe Band Championships.
Streetbiz (street performers festival).
November: Fireworks Display (Glasgow Green).

Gourock

August: International Formula One Class World Yachting Grand Prix.

Inveraray

Mid July: Highland Games.

Islay, Isle of

End May/June: Islay Mod (Bowmore).
End July–August: Rhinns of Islay Celtic Festival.

Jura, Isle of

End May: Isle of Jura Fell Race.

Killin

August, third week: Agricultural Show.

Kilmarnock

June: Kilmarnock and Loudoun Burns Day.
August/September: Kilmarnock and Loudoun Festival of Leisure.
End November: Craft Fair.

Kirkconnel

Mid June: Kirkconnel and Kelloholm Gala.

Kirkcudbright

July–August: Kirkcudbright Summer Festivities.

Lanark
June, first week: 'Perambulation of the Marches'.
June, first/second week: Lanimar Day.

Langholm
End July: Common Riding.

Lockerbie
June, first week: Lockerbie Gala and Riding of the Marches.

Luss
Mid July: Highland Games.

Mabie Forest
Mid December: 'Mabie Fayre'.

Mid Argyll
August, first and second week: Art Show.
August, second week: Agricultural Show.

Moffat
July, second week: Gala Week.
August, second week: South of Scotland Tennis Championships.
End August: Agricultural Show.

Motherwell
June, third week: Scottish Amateur Rowing Association Regatta.
June, fourth week: Scottish Canoe Association Regatta.
End September: Bastables Autumn Fair.
October, first and second week: Music Festival.

Mull, Isle of
April, fourth week: Mull Traditional Music Festival (Tobermory).
July, third week: Tobermory Highland Games.
July, fourth week: Mull Children's Highland Games (Tobermory).
End July–August: West Highland Yachting Week (around Mull and Oban).
October, second week: Mull Car Rally.

New Galloway
July, second week: Gala Week.

New Lanark
September, first week: Victorian Fair.

Newton Stewart
August, first/second week: Forestry Commission Fun Week.

Oban
May, second week: Highlands and Islands Music and Dance Festival.
May, third week: Bruichladdich Islands Peak Race.
May, fourth week: RNLI Raft Race.
June, first week: Oban Provincial Mod.
June–July: Open-air productions at McCaig's Tower.
July, fourth week: The Great Bed Race.
End July–August: West Highland Yachting Week (around Oban and Mull).
August, third/fourth week: Argyllshire Highland Gathering.

Palnackie
End July: Flounder Tramping Championships.

Parton
August, first/second week: Scottish Alternative Games.

Portpatrick
End July: Lifeboat Week.

Port William
End July/August: Carnival Week.

Sanquhar
March/April: Easter Egg Hunt.

Festvals/Events (cont.)

August, second/third week:
Riding of the Marches.

Shotts

June, first week: Highland Games
and West of Scotland Pipe Band
Championships.

Southend

Mid July: Highland Games.

Stewarton

Mid June: Guild Festival Week.

Stirling

End February–April: Scottish
Community Drama Association,
Festival of One-Act Plays.

June, first–third week: Stirling
District Festival.

July, third and fourth weeks: Stirling
Tartan Festival.

August, first and second weeks:
Trossachs Highland Festival.

September, second week: Scottish
National Chrysanthemum and
Dahlia Society Show.

Stranraer

Mid July: Wigtownshire Hunt
Country Fair.

End July/August: Agricultural
Show.

August, second week: Galloway
Games.

Tarbert

End May: McEwan's Scottish Series
Yacht Race.

End July: Tarbert Fair.

September; first week: Flower Show.

Mid–end September: McEwan's
Music Festival.

Thornhill

End May: South of Scotland Field
Sports Fair.

Mid June: 'Summer Solstice Stroll'.

July, second/third week: Horse
Driving Trials (Drumlanrig
Castle).

End July: 'Porridge Oats Chase'.

August, second week: Conservation
Fair.

Tiree, Isle of

End September–October: Wave
Classic Windsurfing Competition.

Troon

September, first/second week: Open
Amateur Golf Tournament.

GALLERIES

Galleries listed below are intended as a quick reference guide only. Galleries which are included as part of a museum are listed under Museums, unless they merit particular mention, in which case there is an entry for both the gallery and the museum.

Ayr

Maclaurin Art Gallery and Rozelle House: Rozelle Park, Monument Road (0292 45447/43708). Converted house and stable block, housing permanent and temporary exhibitions of fine and contemporary art respectively. Photography and crafts are also covered, and in the grounds there are sculptures by Henry Moore.

Campbeltown

The Oystercatcher Crafts and Gallery: 10 Hall Street (0586 553070). Crafts, paintings and glassware.

Castle Douglas

Castle Douglas Art Gallery: Market Street (0557 31643). Temporary exhibitions of art, photography and craft throughout the year and a permanent display of local work.

Drymen

Rowan Gallery: 36 Main Street (0360 60996). Changing exhibitions throughout the year, mostly contemporary, on a wide range of themes.

Dumfries

Gracefield Arts Centre: 28 Edinburgh Road (0387 62084). Collection of over 400 Scottish paintings and regular exhibitions of contemporary art. Also, darkroom, pottery and studios.

Dunblane

Cornerstone Gallery: Cathedral Square (0786 823696). Temporary exhibitions throughout the year.

Glasgow

Full details of Glasgow's many galleries are available in *The Glasgow Galleries Guide*, available from Tourist Information Offices.

Barbizon Gallery: 40 High Street (041–553 1990). Contemporary and modern British painting, with a strong emphasis on young Scottish artists.

Collins Gallery: University of Strathclyde, Richmond Street (041–552 4400 ext 2682/2416). Lively programme of temporary exhibitions, recitals, poetry readings and jazz.

Compass Gallery: 178 West Regent Street (041–221 6370). Glasgow's longest-established contemporary gallery. Monthly exhibitions of paintings, prints and sculpture by Scottish and British artists.

Glasgow Group Gallery: 17 Queens Crescent, St George's Cross (041–332 4924). Run by artists and housed in a listed building, the Glasgow Group has provided a focus for contemporary work in the west of Scotland since 1957. Continually changing exhibitions.

Glasgow Print Studio: 22 King Street (041–552 0704). Contemporary gallery showing monthly exhibitions of original prints, paintings and sculpture by local, national and international artists.

Kelvingrove Art Gallery: Argyle Street (041–357 3929). One of Britain's

Galleries (cont.)

finest collections of British and European paintings.

Kilmarnock

The Dick Institute: Elmbank Avenue (0563 26401). Permanent collection of paintings and touring exhibitions of prints, photographs, pottery, jewellery, textiles and other crafts.

Kirkcudbright

Broughton House: High Street (0557 30437). Home of the Scottish artist E.A. Hornel, now open to the public and housing a permanent exhibition of works by Hornel and other artists. Also, large library with works by Burns and Japanese-style garden.

Harbour Cottage Art Gallery: The Harbour (0557 30207). Temporary exhibitions throughout the year near the harbour.

New Abbey

Brambling Fine Arts: Beeswing Road (0387 76 643). Countryside studios of a local wildlife artist. Original paintings for sale as well as Galloway Glass engraving.

Paisley

Paisley Museum and Art Galleries: High Street, Paisley (041–889 3151). Significant collection of Scottish and contemporary paintings and ceramics (see under Museums).

Stirling

Allan Park Gallery: Allan Park (0786 71411). Temporary exhibitions throughout the year.

Smith Art Gallery and Museum: Dumbarton Road (0786 71917). Temporary exhibitions, often depicting different aspects of Scottish life.

Tighnabruaich

Kyles-Side Painting Centre: Tighnabruaich (0700 811 681/0700 82 257). Gallery, studio, art club and tuition (by arrangement).

GOLF CLUBS/ASSOCIATIONS

Visitors are welcome at the courses listed below, but are requested to phone ahead to check times. Note that many clubs require written applications, particularly for groups, and often with at least 21 days' notice. Full details of clubs are usually available from Tourist Information Offices in the relevant areas.

Arran, Isle of

Brodick Golf Club: Brodick (0770 2349). 18 hole.

Lamlash Golf Club: Lamlash (0770 6296). 18 hole.

Lochranza Golf Course and Putting Green: Lochranza (0770 83 273). 9 hole.

Machrie Golf and Tennis Club: Machrie (0770 86 435). 9 hole.

Shiskine Golf and Tennis Club: Black- waterfoot (0770 86 226). 12 hole.

Whiting Bay Golf Club: Whiting Bay (0770 7487). 18 hole.

Ayr

Belleisle Golf Course: Belleisle Park (0292 41258). 18 hole.

Dalmilling Golf Course: Westwood Crescent (0292 263893). 18 hole.

Seafield Golf Course: Belleisle Park (0292 41258). 18 hole.

Beith

Beith Golf Club: Threepwood Road (05055 3166). 9 hole.

Bellshill

Bellshill Golf Club: Community

Road, Orbiston (0698 745124). 18 hole.

Biggar

Biggar Golf Club: The Park, Broughton Road (0899 20319). 18 hole.

Bothwell

Bothwell Castle Golf Club: Blantyre Road (0698 853177). 18 hole.

Bute, Isle of

Bute Golf Course: Kingarth (contact the secretary, 0770 83648). 9 hole.

Port Bannatyne Golf Course: Port Bannatyne (0700 502009). 13 hole.

Rothesay Golf Club: Canada Hill (0700 502244). 18 hole.

Carluke

Carluke Golf Club: Mauldslie Road, Hallcraig (0555 71070). 18 hole.

Carnwath

Carnwath Golf Club: 1 Main Street (0555 840251). 18 hole.

Cumbrae, Isle of

Millport Golf Club: (0475 530311). 18 hole.

Dollar

Dollar Golf Club: Brewlands House (0259 42400). 18 hole.

Dumfries

Dumfries and County Golf Club: Edinburgh Road (0387 53585). 18 hole.

Dunoon

Cowal Golf Club: Ardenslate Road, Kirn (0369 5673). 18 hole.

Golf Clubs/Associations (cont.)

East Kilbride

East Kilbride Golf Club: Nerston (03552 20913). 18 hole.

Langlands Golf Course: Langlands Road, Auldhouse (03552 24685). 18 hole.

Torrance House Golf Course: Calderglen Country Park, Strathaven Road (03552 48638). 18 hole.

Girvan

Girvan Golf Club: Contact Kyle and Carrick District Council, Knockcushan Street, Girvan (0465 2056). 18 hole.

Glenluce

Wigtownshire County Golf Club: Mains of Park (05813 420). 18 hole.

Hamilton

Strathclyde Park Golf Course: Mote Hill (0698 66155). 9 hole.

Irvine

Glasgow Gailes Club: Gailes (0294 311347). 18 hole.

Irvine Golf Club: Bogside (0294 75979). 18 hole.

Ravenspark Golf Course: Kidsneuk (0294 79550). 18 hole.

Western Gailes Golf Club: Gailes (0294 311357). 18 hole.

Kilbirnie

Kilbirnie Place Golf Club: Largs Road (0505 683398). 18 hole.

Killin

Killin Golf Club: Killin (05672 312). 9 hole.

Kirkcudbright

Kirkcudbright Golf Club: Stirling Crescent (0557 30314). 18 hole.

Kirkhill

Kirkhill Golf Course: Greenlees Road (041–641 3083/8499). 18 hole.

Lanark

Lanark Golf Club: The Moor (0555 2349). 18 hole and 9 hole.

Largs

Largs Golf Club (Kelburn): Irvine Road (0475 673594). 18 hole.

Routenburn Golf Club: Routenburn Road (0475 673230). 18 hole.

Larkhall

Larkhall Golf Club: Burnhead Road (0698 881113). 9 hole.

Leadhills

Leadhills Golf Club: near Biggar (065974 222). 9 hole.

Lesmahagow

Holland Golf Club: Acretophead, Coalburn (0555 893646). 18 hole.

Lockerbie

Lockerbie Golf Club: Corrie Road (057 62 3363). 18 hole.

Maybole

Maybole Golf Course: Maybole (0655 82124). 9 hole.

Moffat

Moffat Golf Club: Coatshill (0683 20020). 18 hole.

Motherwell

Colville Park Golf Club: Jerviston Estate (0698 63017). 18 hole.

Mull, Isle of

Craignure Golf Club: Scallastle, Craignure (06802 370). 9 hole.

Tobermory Golf Club: Tobermory (0688 2020). 9 hole.

New Galloway

New Galloway Golf Club: New Galloway (06443 455). 9 hole.

Newton Stewart

Newton Stewart Golf Club: Kirroughtree Avenue, Minnigaff (0671 2172). 9 hole.

Oban

Glencruitten Golf Club: Glencruitten Road (0631 62868). 18 hole.

Patna

Doon Valley Golf Club: Hillside (0292 531607). 9 hole.

Portpatrick

Portpatrick (Dunskey) Golf Club: Golf Course Road (077681 273). 18 hole and 9 hole.

Prestwick

Prestwick Golf Club: Links Road (0292 77404). 18 hole.

St Cuthbert Golf Club: East Road (0292 77101). 18 hole.

St Nicholas Golf Club: Grangemuir Road (0292 79755). 18 hole.

Rigside

Douglas Water Golf Club: Ayr Road (055588 460). 9 hole.

Rutherglen

Cathkin Braes Golf Club: Cathkin Road (041–634 0650). 18 hole.

Sanquhar

Sanquhar Golf Club: Euchan Course, Blackaddie Road (0659 50577). 9 hole.

Shotts

Shotts Golf Club: Blairhead (0501 22658). 18 hole.

Skelmorlie

Skelmorlie Golf Club: Golf Course Road (0475 520152). 13 hole.

Southerness

Southerness Golf Club: Kirkbean (038788 677). 18 hole.

Stevenston

Ardeer Golf Club: Greenhead (0294 64542). 18 hole.

Auchenharvie Golf Course: On the shore road (0294 603103). 9 hole plus 18 bay floodlit range.

Stranraer

Stranraer Golf Club: Creachmore (0776 87 245). 18 hole.

Strathaven

Strathaven Golf Club: Glasgow Road (0357 20421). 18 hole.

Tarbert

Tarbert Golf Club: Kilberry Road (0880 820565). 9 hole.

Thornhill

Thornhill Golf Club: Blacknest (0848 30546). 18 hole.

Troon

Darley Golf Course: Harling Drive (0292 312464). 18 hole.

Fullarton Golf Course: Harling Drive (0292 312464). 18 hole.

Lochgreen Golf Course: Harling Drive (0292 312464). 18 hole.

Portland Course: (0292 313281). 18 hole.

Royal Troon Golf Club: Craigend Road (0292 311555). 18 hole.

Turnberry

Ailsa Golf Course: Turnberry Hotel (0655 31000). 18 hole.

Arran Golf Course: Turnberry (0655 31370). 18 hole.

Uddingston

Calderbraes Golf Club: 57 Roundknowe Road (0698 813425). 9 hole.

West Kilbride

West Kilbride Golf Club: Fullarton Drive, Seamill (0294 823128). 18 hole.

Wishaw

Wishaw Golf Club: Cleland Road (0698 372869). 18 hole.

HALF-DAY CLOSING

Tuesday
Lockerbie, Clackmannan.

Wednesday
Alva, Annan, Isle of Arran, Ayr, Biggar, Bute, Isle of (Rothesay), Campbeltown, Dalbeattie, Dunoon, Girvan, Gourock, Gretna, Inveraray, Kilmarnock, Kirkconnel (post office and Co-op), Kirkcudbright (some shops on Thursday), Langholm, Moffat, Motherwell, Mull, Isle of, Newton Stewart, Stewarton, Stranraer, Thornhill (post office), Troon.

Thursday
Castle Douglas, Dumfries, Gatehouse of Fleet, Islay, Isle of, Kirkconnel, Kirkcudbright (some shops on Wednesday), Lanark, Oban, Portpatrick, Port William, Sanquhar, Thornhill.

LEISURE/SPORTS CENTRES

These include swimming pools, ski slopes, bowling alleys, ice rinks, general athletics grounds and gymnasia.

Alloa

Alloa Leisure Bowl: Park Way (0259 723527). Swimming pool, squash, snooker, indoor bowling, Turkish bath and sauna.

Clackmannan Road Sports Centre: Clackmannan Road (0259 723527). Sports halls, games facilities and multi-gym.

Annan

Annan Swimming Pool: St John's Road (0461 204773/203311).

Everholm Sports Complex: Battery Street (0461 205874). Putting, swingball, table tennis, athletics track and fitness room.

Ayr

Ayrshire Curlers and Ice Rink: 9 Limekiln Road (0292 263024). Curling and skating.

Centrum: Ayr Road, Prestwick Toll (0292 671717). Scotland's first multi-purpose events area, including an Olympic-size ice rink.

Bridge of Allan

Sunnylaw Country Club: Pendreich Road (0786 832948). Swimming pool, sauna, steam room, sunbeds and fitness room.

Bute, Isle of

The Moat Centre: Stuart Street, Rothesay (0700 503696). Community Education Centre with indoor recreational facilities.

Swimming Pool: High Street, Rothesay (0700 504300). Swimming pool, sauna and fitness facilities.

Castle Douglas

Swimming Pool: Market Street (0556 2745). With sauna and sunbed.

Lochside Park: next to Carlingwark Loch, bottom of town (Stewartry District Council, 0557 30291). Rowing boats and canoes for hire, putting, play area, squash, tennis club and bowling green.

Coatbridge

Monklands Time Capsule: Bank Street (0236 31 181). Recently opened 'state of the art' leisure water and ice facilities.

Cumbernauld

Tryst Sports Centre: Town Centre, (0236 728138). Swimming pool, sauna, games hall and squash courts.

Dalbeattie

Colliston Park: Mill Street (Stewartry District Council, 0557 30291). Paddle boats, putting, trampolines, tennis and play area.

Dalmellington

Doon Valley Indoor Swimming Pool: Ayr Road (0292 550665).

Darvel

The Gavin Hamilton Sports Centre: Jamieson Road (0560 21949). Badminton, fitness training and a range of sporting activities.

Dumbarton

Meadow Sports Centre: Meadow Road (0389 34094). Swimming pool, slides, sports hall, fitness room, aerobics, badminton and a crèche.

Dumfries

Swimming Pool: Greensands (0387 52908).

David Keswick Athletics Centre: Marchmount (0387 69423). Badminton, table tennis, short mat bowls and athletics.

Fintry

Fintry Sports and Recreation Club: Fintry (follow signs for Culcreuch Castle) (036086 297). Indoor bowling, table tennis, squash.

Glasgow

Bishopbriggs Sports Centre: 147 Balmuildy Road, Bishopbriggs (041–772 6391). Swimming pool and a variety of sporting activities in a number of sports halls.

Crownpoint Sports Complex: 183 Crownpoint Road (041–554 8274). Outdoor sports complex with two artificial turf parks, blaes grass, track and athletics park.

Kelvin Hall International Sports Arena: Argyle Street (041–357 2525). Extensive facilities for the casual user or competitive athlete.

Helensburgh

Swimming Pool: Pier Head (0436 72224). Pool, sunbeds, gymnasium.

Irvine

Magnum Leisure Centre: Harbourside (0294 78381). Swimming pool.

Killin

Killin Bowling Club: Killin (05672 330). Visitors welcome; phone ahead to organize a time.

Kilmarnock

Galleon Centre: 99 Titchfield Street (0563 24014). Large leisure centre offering a comprehensive range of sports and amusements, from aqua-discos to yoga.

The Hunter Centre: Ardbeg Avenue (0563 41350). Badminton, fitness training and a range of sporting activities.

Kirkconnel

Hillview Leisure Centre: Kirkland Drive (0659 67777). Games hall, badminton, carpet bowls, fitness room, sunbeds, putting green and a crèche.

Menstrie

Dumyat Leisure Centre: Menstrie (0259 213131). Sports hall and games facilities.

Moffat

Beechgrove Sports Centre: Edinburgh Road (0683 20697). All indoor sports offered.

Motherwell

Aquatec: Menteith Road (0698 76464). Ice rink, leisure pool, health room, gym and video arcade.

Newmilns

Newmilns Dry Ski Slope: High Street (0560 22320). Skiing all year round.

Paisley

Lagoon Leisure Centre: Mill Street (041–889 4000). Leisure pool, sauna, steam room, jacuzzis and sunbeds.

Prestwick

Prestwick Golf Range: Monkton Road (0292 79849). Golf driving range.

Leisure/Sports Centres (cont.)

Prestwick Indoor Bowling Club:
Bellevue Road (0292 77802). Visitors
welcome, beginners and experts.

Stirling

Rainbow Slides Leisure Centre:
Goosecroft Road (0786 62521).
Swimming pool, slides, massage,
sauna, steam room, sunbeds,
weights.

Hollywood Bowl: 22 Forth Street
(0786 63915). Ten-pin bowling.

Stirling Ice Rink: Williamfield
(0786 50389).

Indoor Bowling Centre: Forth Street
(0786 63168).

Stranraer

Wig Bay: (0776 2151 ext 244,
Wigtown District Council).
RYA-approved sailing courses
for dinghies and windsurfing on
Loch Ryan.

Ryan Leisure Centre: Fairhurst Road
(0776 3535). Games hall, badminton,
tennis, volleyball, netball, fitness
room and sauna.

LIBRARIES

Annan

Annan Library: Charles Street (046 12 202809).

Auchinleck

Auchinleck Branch Library: Community Centre, Well Road (0290 22829).

Ayr

Carnegie Library: Main Street (0292 269141).

Bellshill

Bellshill Cultural Centre: John Street (0698 841831).

Bothwell

Bothwell Library: Main Street (0698 853150).

Bute, Isle of

Moat Centre: Stuart Street, Rothesay (0700 503266).

Campbeltown

Campbeltown Library: Hall Street (0586 552367).

Carluke

Carluke Library: Carnwath Road (0555 72134).

Castle Douglas

Castle Douglas Library: Markethill, King Street (0556 2643).

Catrine

Catrine Library: A.M. Brown Institute (0290 51717).

Cumnock

Cumnock Library: Millbank (0290 22804).

Netherthird Library: Ryderston Drive, Netherthird (0290 23806).

Dalbeattie

Dalbeattie Library: 23 High Street (0556 610898).

Dalmellington

Bellsbank Library: Primary School, Craiglea Crescent (0292 551057).

Dalmellington Library: Townhead (0292 550159).

Dalrymple

Dalrymple Library: Barbieston Road (029 256 511).

Dumfries

Ewart Library: Catherine Street (0387 53820).

Lochside Library: Lochside Road (0387 68751).

Gatehouse of Fleet

Gatehouse of Fleet Library: High Street (0557 814646).

Girvan

Girvan Library: Montgomerie Street (0465 2813).

Glasgow (city centre)

Bishopbriggs Library: Kirkintilloch Road, Bishopbriggs (041–772 4513).

Mitchell Library: North Street (041–221 7030). Largest public reference library in Europe.

Hamilton

Hamilton Library: Cadzow Street (0698 282323).

Libraries (cont.)

Kilmarnock

The Dick Institute: Elmbank Avenue
(0563 26401).

Kirkcudbright

Kirkcudbright Library: High Street
(0557 31240).

Lanark

Lanark Library: Hope Street
(0555 61331 ext 246).

Langholm

Langholm Library: Charles Street Old
(03873 80040).

Leadhills

Allan Ramsay Library: (0659 74326;
see under Museums).

Lockerbie

Lockerbie Library: High Street
(057 62 3380).

Mauchline

Mauchline Library: The Loan
(0290 50824).

Moffat

Moffat Library: High Street
(0683 20952).

Motherwell

Motherwell Library: Hamilton Road
(0698 51311).

Muirkirk

Muirkirk Library: Burns Avenue
(0290 61505).

New Cumnock

New Cumnock Library: Community
Centre, The Castle (0290 38710).

Ochiltree

Ochiltree Library: Main Street
(029 07 425).

Patna

Patna Library: Doonside Avenue
(0292 531538).

Prestwick

Prestwick Library: Kyle Street
(0292 76769).

Sanquhar

Sanquhar Library: High Street
(0659 50626).

Thornhill

Thornhill Library: Townhead Street
(0848 30654).

Troon

Troon Library: South Beach
(0292 315352).

Whithorn

Whithorn Library: St John Street
(098 85 406).

Wigtown

Wigtown Library: Duncan Park
(098 84 3329).

LOCAL MEDIA

NEWSPAPERS

Dumfries and Galloway

Dumfriesshire Newspapers: 96 High Street, Annan (0461 202417/202532). Publishes **Annandale Herald** (Thursday); **Moffat News** (Thursday); **Dumfries Courier** (Friday); **Annandale Observer** (Friday).

Dumfries and Galloway Standard (Wednesday and Friday) and **Galloway News** (Thursday): Scottish and Universal Newspapers, Glasgow Road, Dumfries (0387 55252).

Eskdale and Liddesdale Advertiser: Eastons Entry, Langholm (03873 80 486).

Galloway Gazette: Victoria Lane, Newton Stewart (0671 2503).

South-West Advertiser: 21 St John's Street, Stranraer (0776 2266).

Wigtown Free Press: St Andrew's Street, Stranraer (0776 2551).

Strathclyde

Argyllshire Advertiser: 44 Argyll Street, Lochgilphead (0546 2345).

Arran Banner: Brodick, Isle of Arran (0770 242).

Ayr Advertiser: Fort Street, Ayr (0292 267631).

Ayrshire Post: Nile Court, 154 High Street, Ayr (0292 261111).

Buteman: 10 Castle Street, Rothesay, Isle of Bute (0700 512931).

Campbeltown Courier: Main Street, Campbeltown (0586 554646).

Carrick Gazette: 32 Dalrymple Street, Girvan (0465 2688).

East Kilbride News: East Kilbride (035 52 65000).

Hamilton and Carluke Advertiser: Bloomgate, Lanark (0555 3063).

The Herald (formerly the *Glasgow Herald*) and **Evening Times:** 195 Albion Street, Glasgow (041–552 6255).

Lanark Gazette: Wellgate, Lanark (0555 3937).

Motherwell Times: Motherwell (0698 64611).

MAGAZINES

Dumfries and Galloway

Tourist Express: AGT Newspapers, 32 Lowther Street, Carlisle (0228 41151). Information, dates and useful addresses for visitors to south-west Scotland, the Borders, Northumbria and Cumbria. Available from newsagents and Tourist Information Centres.

RADIO

Central

CentreSound Radio: John Player Building, Stirling Enterprise Park, Kerse Road, Stirling (0786 51188). 96.7 FM.

Dumfries and Galloway

BBC Radio Solway: Elsbank, Lovers Walk, Dumfries (0387 68008). 93.97 FM (94.7 FM).

West Sound Radio: Campbell House, Bankend Road, Dumfries (0387 50999). 97.2 FM.

Strathclyde

East End Radio, The Greater Easterhouse Business Centre, Unit 16, 19 Blairtummock Road, Queenslie Industrial Estate, Glasgow (041–774 5335). 103.5 FM.

Local Media (cont.)

Radio Clyde: Clydebank Business Park, Clydebank, Glasgow (041–941 1111). MW: 1152 kHz/261m; VHF: 102.5 MHz.

West Sound Radio: 54 Holmston Road, Ayr (0292 283662/284111). MW: 1035 kHz/290m, 96.7 FM, 97.2 FM.

TELEVISION

Dumfries and Galloway

BBC Television: Dumfries, Elsbank, Lovers Walk, Dumfries (0387 68008).

Strathclyde

BBC Television: Broadcasting House, Queen Margaret Drive, Glasgow (041–330 2345).

Scottish Television plc: Cowcaddens, Glasgow (041–332 9999).

MUSEUMS

The list of museums below represents a cross-section of those found throughout the area and is intended as a quick reference guide only. Full details of museums in specific locations are obtainable from the relevant Tourist Information Office. Museums of special interest are included in the Gazetteer.

Airdrie

Weaver's Cottage Museum: Wellwynd (0236 47712). Reconstructed weaver's cottage and exhibition area of local history.

Alloa

Alloa Museum: Speirs Centre, Primrose Street (0259 213131). Temporary exhibitions, artefacts, local artwork and crafts.

Arran, Isle of

Isle of Arran Heritage Museum: Rosaburn, Brodick (0770 2636). Exhibition depicting island life up until the 1920s.

Auchinleck

The Boswell Museum: Parish Church (0290 20757). Artefacts relating to Sir James Boswell, a famous Scots man of letters and biographer of Dr Johnson. Open by appointment.

Biggar

Gladstone Court Museum: A702 North Back Road (0899 21050). Reproduction Victorian street with shops, bank, telephone exchange and schoolroom.

Greenhill Covenanter's House Burn Braes (0899 21050). 17th-century farmhouse containing displays, furniture and relics of Covenanting times.

Moat Park Heritage Centre: Biggar town centre (0899 21050). Local history museum, including exhibits dating from 6000 years ago to the present day.

Bute, Isle of

Bute Museum: Stuart Street, Rothesay (0700 502248). Exhibitions on the history, natural history and archaeology of the Isle of Bute (see also under Organizations).

Winter Garden Visitor Centre: Victoria Street, Rothesay (0700 502487). Display relating to the island's heritage. Also containing a restored 1920s seaside theatre and a new cinema.

Callander

Rob Roy and Trossachs Visitor Centre: Ancaster Square (0877 30342). Opened in 1990, exhibitions telling the story of the famous Scottish outlaw Rob Roy.

Castle Douglas

Laurieston Weather Centre: near Castle Douglas (06445 264). Displays of weather-recording instruments, satellite technology and a computerized weather quiz.

Crawfordjohn

Crawfordjohn Heritage Venture: (0555 82437). Exhibitions on country life, wildlife exhibits, photographs, Covenanting tales and agricultural memorabilia.

Cumbernauld

Cumbernauld Museum: Ardenlea House, The Wynd (0236 735077).

Museums (cont.)

Social history museum portraying the origins and development of Cumbernauld, based at the District Council Museum offices.

Cumbrae, Isle of

Marine Biological Station and Museum: (0475 530581/2). Opened for scientific research in 1887 and extended in 1903, now with an interesting aquarium.

Museum of the Cumbraes: Garrison House, Millport (0475 530741). Small local history museum with regular changing exhibitions, housed in a historic building.

Cumnock

Baird Institute Museum: Lugar Street (contact library headquarters: 0290 22111). Museum established with funds left by John Baird, a local draper who died in 1888. Collections of Ayrshire embroidery, Cumnock pottery and Mauchline ware.

Dalmellington

Scottish Industrial Railway Centre: Minnivey Colliery (0292 531144). Rolling stock, steam engines, diesel locomotives, museum of railway relics and a chance to ride behind a steam locomotive.

Dumbarton

Denny Ship Model Experimental Tank: Castle Street (0389 63444). The history of ship design.

Dumfries

Camera Obscura: Dumfries Museum, The Observatory (0387 53374). Camera Obscura at the local museum, situated in and around the 18th-century windmill tower on Corbelly Hill and offering panoramic views of the surrounding countryside. Dates from 1836.

Crichton Royal Museum: Easterbrook Hall, Crichton Royal Hospital, Bankend Road (0387 55301 ext 2360). Displays on over 200 years of mental patient care in this area of Scotland. Artwork, operating theatre, library and stained glass.

Dumfries and Galloway Aviation Museum: Former Control Tower, Heathall Industrial Estate (0387 710491 daytime Monday–Friday, 0387 65957 evenings). Open at weekends, aviation artefacts including aircraft and engines from 1914 to the present day. Situated on the site of a former RAF airfield and run by a team of enthusiasts.

Old Bridge House: Mill Road (0387 56904). Dumfries's oldest house, built into the 15th-century Devorgilla Bridge, now houses a museum of everyday life.

Shambellie House Museum of Costume: New Abbey, Dumfries (038785 375). Costumes and accessories from throughout the ages.

Dunblane

Cathedral Museum: Dunblane Cathedral (0786 824254). Local and church history.

Gatehouse of Fleet

Skyreburn Aquarium: by Gatehouse of Fleet (067182 403/204). Over 50 species of local freshwater fish and animals, displays and underwater photographs.

Glasgow

Dome of Discovery: South Rotunda, Govan Road (041–427 1792). The world of science explained through hands-on exhibits.

Museum of the 602 (City of Glasgow) Squadron: Queen Elizabeth Avenue, Hillington (041–882 6201 ext 105). Photographs and memorabilia of Glasgow's most famous squadron.

Police Museum: Strathclyde Police, 173 Pitt Street (041–204 2626). Displays relating to the Strathclyde Police, by appointment only.

Regimental Museum of the Royal Highland Fusiliers: 518 Sauchiehall Street (041–332 0961). Military memorabilia relating to the regiment's 300-year history.

Rutherglen Museum of Local History: King Street, Rutherglen (041–647 0837). Continually changing displays relating to the former royal burgh of Rutherglen.

St Mungo Heritage Centre: Wellpark Brewery, Duke Street (041–552 6552 ext 3020). Guided tours around one of Glasgow's famous landmarks, which has been brewing beer for over 100 years.

Thomas Muir Museum: Bishopbriggs Library, Kirkintilloch Road (041–772 4513). Exhibition about the life and work of Thomas Muir, the radical reformer.

Glenluce

Glenluce Motor Museum: Glenluce (05813 534). Vintage cars, bikes and 'Motorbilia'.

Greenock

Custom House: Princes Pier (0475 26331). 'Smuggler's' exhibition covering the history and work of Customs and Excise, housed in what is reputed to be one of the finest custom house quay

buildings in Britain, built in 1818 by William Burn.

McLean Museum and Art Gallery: Union Street (0475 23741). Exhibitions on local history, ethnography and natural history, as well as paintings by a number of leading Scottish artists.

Hamilton

Cameronian Museum: Mote Hill, off Muir Street (0698 285382). Military museum with exhibitions relating to the Scottish Rifles and Covenanting movement, housed in the Duke of Hamilton's former riding school.

Hamilton Museum: 129 Muir Street (0698 283981). Local history and transport museum in a 17th-century coaching inn.

Irvine

Glasgow Vennel Museum: 4 & 10 Glasgow Vennel (0294 75059). Exhibitions on Burns and a gallery of temporary exhibitions, ranging from local groups to international artists.

Irvine Burns Club and Museum, see under Organizations.

Scottish Maritime Museum: Laird Forge, Gattries Road (0294 78283). Maritime history exhibition and a number of historic vessels, including the puffer *Spartan* on board which conditions have not changed for 40 years.

Islay, Isle of

Museum of Islay Life: Port Charlotte (049685 358). Exhibits relating to the life and times of Islay people.

Kilbirnie

Stables Museum, see under Organizations.

Museums (cont.)
Kilmarnock

Burns Monument and Museum:
Kay Park, Grassyard Road (0563
34580/26401). More of the life and
times of Burns.

The Dick Institute: Elmbank Avenue
(0563 26401). Exhibits on geology,
natural history, engineering,
archaeology and local history.

Kilsyth

Colzium Museum: Colzium Lennox
Estate (0236 735077). Local history
museum housed in a Victorian
mansion.

Kilsyth Heritage Museum: Kilsyth
Library, Burngreen (0236 823146).
Social history of the Kilsyth area in
the 19th and 20th centuries.

Kirkcudbright

Stewartry Museum: St Mary Street
(0557 31643). Displays of local, social
and natural history.

Kirkintilloch

Auld Kirk Museum: Cowgate
(041–775 1185). Temporary
exhibitions including work of local
clubs and societies.

Barony Chambers: The Cross (041–775
1185). Local history museum with
displays on the social and industrial
history of Kirkintilloch and the
surrounding area.

Langholm

**Craigcleuch: Scottish Explorers
Museum:** Two miles north-west of
Langholm on B709 (03873 80137).
Collection of ethnic art and artefacts
from around the world.

Largs

Christian Heritage Museum:
Benedictine Monastery,

5 Mackerston Place (0475 687320).
History of Christian monasticism
in Britain and south-west Scotland.
Advisable to phone ahead and check
opening times.

**Largs and District Historical
Society Museum:** Kirkgate House,
Manse Court (0475 687081).
Old photographs and records,
Ayrshire embroidery, pottery and
Mauchline ware.

Leadhills

Allan Ramsay Library: (0659 74326).
Oldest subscription library in
Britain, established in 1741 and
dedicated to Allan Ramsay, a native
of Leadhills and noted writer and
poet. Rare books, old mining records
and maps.

Lochwinnoch

Lochwinnoch Community Museum:
High Street (0505 842615).
Community museum reflecting the
history of agriculture, industry and
village life.

Mauchline

Burns House Museum: Castle Street
(0290 50045). Museum dedicated to
the life of Robert Burns, who started
married life with Jean Armour in
this room in 1788. Visitors should
check in advance whether the
museum is open.

Moffat

Moffat Museum: Churchgate (0683
20868). Local museum telling the
history of Moffat, from sheep town
to spa town.

Moniaive

Maxwelton House: near Moniaive
(08482 385). Museum and other

attractions at the birthplace of Annie Laurie.

Newton Stewart

The Museum: York Road (0671 2106/2472). Large local, social and natural history exhibition from around the area.

Oban

McCaig Museum: Corran Hall (0631 64211 ext 221). Small local history exhibition.

Paisley

Paisley Museum: High Street (041–889 3151). Collection of Paisley shawls, the history of the Paisley pattern and the development of weaving techniques in a building built in 1870 in Greek Ionic style (see under Galleries).

Sma' Shot Cottages: Old Paisley Society, 11/17 George Place (041–889 0530/041–812 2513). Fully restored and furnished Victorian artisan's house; exhibition room of photographs and artefacts of local interest.

Portpatrick

'Little Wheels' Toy Transport Display and Model Railway: 6 Hill Street (077681 536). Toys, miniature transport, dolls and a much celebrated model railway.

Ruthwell

Savings Banks Museum: 6½ miles west of Annan (0387 87640). History of the savings banks, from their beginning in this building in 1810 to the present day.

Saltcoats

North Ayrshire Museum: Kirkgate (0294 64174). General history of the area and specific exhibits on Saltcoats, Stevenston and Ardrossan.

Sanquhar

Sanquhar Museum: The Old Tolbooth (0659 50186). Visitor centre with local history displays in a building dating from 1735.

Stranraer

Stranraer Museum: George Street (0776 5088). Local history, farming and archaeological displays. Also fine art and natural history exhibitions, and the **Ross Room**, dedicated to the Arctic explorer Sir John Ross (1777–1856) and his nephew James Clark Ross.

Strathaven

John Hastie Museum: Threestanes Road, near Strathaven Park (03552 43652). Weaving and ceramics displays and relics from Covenanting times.

Taynuilt

Bonawe Ironworks: by Taynuilt (031–244 3101). Founded in 1753, the most complete remaining charcoal-fired ironworks. Displays and exhibitions.

Thornhill

Drumlanrig Castle: (0848 30248). As well as the many treasures housed in the Dumfriesshire home of the Duke of Buccleuch and Queensberry, there is also a **Cycle Museum** here.

Wanlockhead

Museum of Scottish Lead Mining: Goldscaur Row (0659 74387). Period cottages, unique minerals, miners' library, beam engine

Museums (cont.)

and underground exploration at
Scotland's highest village.

West Kilbride

West Kilbride Museum Society: Arthur
Street (0294 822987). History of
the area in exhibitions containing
dresses from Hunterston Estate
Collection, Ayrshire lace and
embroidery, trades and crafts tools,
dolls and toys.

NIGHTLIFE

The venues listed below are those which are known 'night-time spots'. Away from larger towns and cities it becomes more difficult to pin down regular venues but, as a guideline for entertainment-seekers, if you're in a more rural area, see if local hotels are hosting events or if they have an information board. Tourist Information Centres may also have details.

Ayr

Bobby Jones Disco: Burns Statue Square (0292 28049). Disco.

Club de Mar Nightclub: Arthur Street (0292 611136). Disco.

Squires Disco: Ayrshire and Galloway Hotel, Killoch Place (0292 262626).

Elms Court Hotel: Miller Road (0292 264191). Occasional dinner-dances.

Gartferry Hotel: Racecourse Road (0292 262768). Occasional dinner-dances, live jazz.

The Abbotsford Hotel: Corsehill Road (0292 261506). Folk music.

County Hotel: Wellington Square (0292 263368). Country and western evenings. Check in advance which evenings are best for live music.

Girvan

Jesters Nightclub: 35a Bridge Street (0465 2757). Disco and nightclub.

Kings Arms Hotel: Dalrymple Street (0465 3322) holds occasional dinner-dances.

Glasgow

Cotton Club: Scott Street (041–332 0712). Live music and disco.

Follys: 193 Pitt Street (041–332 7322). Disco.

Fury Murray's: 96 Maxwell Street (041–221 6511). Disco.

The Mayfair: 490 Sauchiehall Street (041–332 3872). Recently renovated disco.

Peggy Sue's: 46 West George Street (041–332 3000). Popular disco/'nightspot'.

Sub Club: Jamaica Street (041–248 4600). Live music and disco.

Victoria's: 92 Sauchiehall Street (041–332 1444). Restaurant, cocktail bar and disco.

Kilmarnock

Hippodrome (Scotland) Nightclub: 1 West George Street (0563 21210). Open Wednesday–Sunday.

KA's Disco: 108–112 John Finnie Street (0563 25706). Open Friday and Saturday, popular local disco.

Parkers Discoteque: The Foregate (0563 33676). Open Friday, Saturday and some Sundays.

Prestwick

Towans Hotel: Powmill Road (0292 77831). Holds occasional dinner-dances.

ORGANIZATIONS

The organizations included here have been chosen to cover those areas, places and subjects which are likely to be of most interest to the visitor. Scotland has many hundreds of local organizations which, as well as providing interesting information about their area, are also a good way of meeting local people. Tourist Information Offices usually carry some details of organizations, as do local libraries (listed above).

Arran, Isle of

Arran Angling Association: contact the Tourist Office (address below). Permits available to fish association waters.

Ayr

Alloway Burns Club: contact Mr Glass, 31 Glenconner Road (0292 261355).

Ayrshire Arts Festival and **Robert Burns Festival Associations**: c/o 30 Miller Road, Ayr (0292 262821).

Ayrshire Music Festival Committee: contact W. Robertson Reddick, 22 St Andrews Street, Ayr (0292 267052).

Biggar

Biggar Museum Trust: Moat Park (0899 21050). Details of four museums in the Biggar area.

Bute, Isle of

Buteshire Natural History Society: The Museum, Stuart Street, Rothesay (0700 502248). Working to preserve the island's history.

Carsphairn

Carsphairn Heritage Group: Smittons, Dalry (06446 206). Offering details of Carsphairn heritage trails, local signposted hill, forest and riverside walks and drives in the upland area around Carsphairn village.

Galloway

Galloway Craft Guild: Mr C. Donovan, Secretary, Parton Mill, Castle Douglas (06447 264). Promoting members' work through exhibitions and advertising. Offers a full list and map of craft workshops, details of activities and information on how to join.

Glasgow

Charles Rennie Mackintosh Society: Headquarters, 870 Garscube Road (041–946 6600). Information centre, reference library and shop in the only church to be designed by Charles Rennie Mackintosh.

Scottish Music Information Service: 1 Bowmont Gardens (041–334 6393). Promotes Scottish music and composers – historical, contemporary, classical and traditional. Free information service, monthly news-sheet and library facilities.

Irvine

Irvine Burns Club: 28a Eglinton Street (0294 74511). The oldest continuous Burns Club in the world, founded in 1826. The club's museum is open by arrangement (call the number above) and contains a collection of original Burns manuscripts prepared for the Kilmarnock edition of his poems (1786).

Islay, Isle of

Islay Festival: Information Centre, Port Ellen (0496 2413). Details of the community festival; local and professional musicians, whisky-tasting, concerts, ceilidhs and dances.

Rhinns of Islay Celtic Festival Society: Port Charlotte (049 685 422). Details of the annual festival, including Gaelic and Celtic music and ceilidhs, workshops and whisky-tasting.

Kilbirnie

Garnock Valley Heritage Society: Main Street (0505 683445). Local group working to preserve the history of the town of Kilbirnie. They have established the Stables Museum, housed in the Walker Hall, one of Kilbirnie's most historic buildings, which contains exhibits on local life from the past 150 years.

Leadhills

Lowther's Railway Society Ltd: The Station (0573 23691). Railway

preservation society open to the public on Sundays.

Stirling

Ochil Craft Association: (0324 823142). Details of over 50 craft workers throughout the area.

Troon

Ayrshire Railway Preservation Group: contact Mr G. Thomson, Secretary, 4 Kyle Crescent, Loans (0292 313579).

Royal Scottish Country Dance Society (Ayr Branch): contact Mrs E. Carlyle, 14 Harling Drive (0292 313615).

THEATRES/CONCERT HALLS

Ayr

Borderline Theatre Company: North Harbour Street (0292 281010). Innovative theatre group, plays, reading and workshops in a studio theatre.

Civic Theatre: Craigie Road (0292 264639). Local productions.

Gaiety Theatre: Carrick Street (0292 264630). Touring productions, music, concerts.

Biggar

Biggar Little Theatre: Broughton Road (0899 20631). Venue of Purves Puppets, complete Victorian theatre in miniature, puppet plays, guided tours, exhibition and outdoor Victorian games.

Bute, Isle of

Rothesay Pavilion: Argyle Street, Rothesay (0700 504250). Multi-purpose entertainment, sports and conference venue.

Cumbernauld

Cumbernauld Theatre: Kildrum, Cumbernauld (0236 737235). Drama, dance, music and cabaret.

East Kilbride

The Village Theatre: Maxwell Drive (03552 48669). Local and touring productions.

Glasgow

Citizen's Theatre: Gorbals Street (041–429 0022). Innovative repertory theatre.

City Halls: Candleriggs (041–227 5511). Music of all types.

Glasgow Royal Concert Hall: 2 Sauchiehall Street (041–332 6633). Latest addition to Glasgow's theatre and concert scene, opened in 1991 and home to the Royal Scottish National Orchestra.

Glasgow's 'Grand Ole Opry': 2/4 Govan Road (041–429 5396). Country and western entertainment Friday–Sunday.

Henry Wood Hall: Claremont Street (041–226 3868). Concert hall in a former church.

Kings Theatre: Bath Street (041–227 5511). Drama, popular productions, music and amateur shows.

Mitchell Theatre: Granville Street (041–227 5511). Amateur drama, lectures and meetings.

Pavilion Theatre: Renfield Street (041–332 1846). Variety, pop concerts and pantomime.

Royal Scottish Academy of Music and Drama: 100 Renfrew Street (041–332 5057). Varied programme of international performances, festival theatre and student recitals.

Scottish Exhibition and Conference Centre: Finnieston (041–248 3000). Pop concerts, exhibitions, displays and fashion shows.

Theatre Royal: Hope Street (041–332 9000). Home of Scottish Opera and regular host to Scottish Ballet, the National Theatre and international performances.

Tramway: 25 Albert Drive (041–227 5511). Opera, drama and dance.

Tron Theatre: 63 Trongate (041–552 4267). Contemporary Scottish and international theatre.

Greenock

Greenock Arts Guild Theatre: Campbell Street (0475 23038).

Theatre and gallery hosting touring productions and local arts organizations.

Kilmarnock

Palace Theatre: 9 Green Street (0563 23590). Variety, dance, music, drama and pantomime.

Motherwell

Motherwell Civic Theatre and Concert Hall: Civic Centre (0698 67515). Drama, musicals and concerts.

Mull, Isle of

Mull Little Theatre: Dervaig, Tobermory (06884 267). Britian's smallest theatre, in a converted cow byre. Varied productions with two or more actors.

Oban

Corran Halls: Esplanade (0631 64046). Local and touring productions. Some performances also at the Highland Theatre (see under **Cinemas**).

Paisley

Paisley Arts Centre: New Street (041–887 1010). Converted 18th-century church, performing arts and works by local artists.

Shotts

Henderson Theatre: Kirk Road (0501 21826). Local and touring productions.

Stirling

MacRobert Arts Centre: University of Stirling (0786 73171). The main theatre in this area of Scotland: touring and local productions, pantomimes, musicals, classical concerts and opera.

Strathaven

Town Mills Arts Centre: Town Centre (contact Lanark Tourist Information, address at end). Theatre and arts centre.

TOURIST INFORMATION

Area Tourist Boards

Arran, Isle of, Tourist Board: The Pier, Brodick KA27 8AU (0770 2401).

Ayrshire Tourist Board: Suite 1005, Prestwick Airport, Prestwick KA9 2PL (0292 79000).

Bute, Isle of, Tourist Board: The Pier, Rothesay PA20 9AQ (0700 502151).

Clyde Valley Tourist Board: Horsemarket, Ladyacre Road, Lanark ML11 7LQ (0555 2544).

Dumfries and Galloway Tourist Board: Campbell House, Bankend Road, Dumfries DG1 4TH (0387 50434).

Dunoon and Cowal Tourist Board: 7 Alexandra Parade, Dunoon PA23 8AB (0369 3755).

Forth Valley Tourist Board: Burgh Halls, The Cross, Linlithgow, West Lothian EH49 7AH (0506 844600).

Greater Glasgow Tourist Board: 39 St Vincent Place, Glasgow G1 2ER (041–204 4400).

Loch Lomond, Stirling and Trossachs Tourist Board: 41 Dumbarton Road, Stirling FK8 2QQ (0786 75019).

Mid Argyll, Kintyre and Islay Tourist Board: MacKinnon House, The Pier, Campbeltown PA28 6EF (0586 552056).

Oban, Mull and District Tourist Board: Albany Street, Oban PA34 4AR (0631 63122).

Local Information Centres

Tourist Information Centres in main towns are usually open all year. Those in smaller towns, such as Dalbeattie and Langholm, and subsidiary offices, such as those at motorway service areas, are mostly open from April to October, although a small handful are just from May to August/September. As a general guideline, offices located in town car parks, libraries or museums are open for the summer season only.

Aberfoyle: Main Street (08772 352).

Ardrossan: Ferry Terminal Building, Ardrossan Harbour (0294 601063).

Arran, Isle of: The Pier, Brodick (0770 2140).
Lochranza (0770 83 320).

Ayr: 39 Sandgate (0292 284196).

Balloch: Balloch Road (0389 53533).

Biggar: 155 High Street (0899 21066).

Bute, Isle of: 15 Victoria Street, Rothesay (0700 502151).

Callander: Rob Roy and Trossachs Visitor Centre, Ancaster Square (0877 30342).

Campbeltown: Mackinnon House, The Pier (0586 552056).

Castle Douglas: Markethill (0556 2611).

Cumbrae, Isle of: Stuart Street, Millport (0475 530753).

Cumnock: Town Hall, Glaisnock Street (0290 23058).

Dalbeattie: Town Hall (0556 610117).

Dalmellington: Ayr Road (0292 550145).

Dumbarton: Milton, by Dumbarton (0389 42306).

Dumfries: Whitesands (0387 53862).

Dunblane: Stirling Road (0786 824428).

Dunoon: 7 Alexandra Parade (0369 3785).

Gatehouse of Fleet: Car Park (0557 814 212).

Girvan: Bridge Street (0465 4950).

Glasgow: 35 St Vincent Place
(041–204 4400).
Glasgow Airport (041–848 4440).

Gourock: Pierhead (0475 39467).

Greenock: Municipal Buildings,
23 Clyde Square (0475 24400).

Gretna Green: Annan Road
(0461 37834).

Helensburgh: The Clock Tower
(0436 72642).

Inveraray: Front Street (0499 2063).

Islay, Isle of: Bowmore (049 681 254).

Killin: Main Street (05672 254).

Kilmarnock: 62 Bank Street
(0563 39090).

Kirkcudbright: Harbour Square
(0557 30494).

Lanark: Horsemarket, Ladyacre Road
(0555 61661).

Langholm: High Street (03873 80976).

Largs: Promenade (0475 673765).

Lochgilphead: Lochnell Street
(0546 2344).

Mauchline: National Burns Memorial
Tower, Kilmarnock Road
(0290 51916).

Maybole: Culzean Country Park
(06556 293).

Moffat: Churchgate (0683 20620).

Motherwell: The Library, Hamilton
Road (0698 51311).

Mull, Isle of: Tobermory (0688 2182).

New Cumnock: Town Hall
(0290 38581).

Newton Stewart: Dashwood Square
(0671 2431).

Oban: Argyll Square (0631 63122).

Paisley: Town Hall, Abbey Close
(041–889 0711).

Prestwick: Boydfield Gardens
(0292 79946).
Prestwick Airport, BAA Information
Desk (0292 79822).

Sanquhar: Tolbooth, High Street
(0659 50185).

Stirling: 41 Dumbarton Road
(0786 75019).
Broad Street (0786 79901).

Stranraer: Port Rodie Car Park
(0776 2595).

Tarbet (Loch Lomond):
A82 (03062 260).

Tarbert: Harbour Street
(0880 820429).

Tillicoultry: The Clock Mill, Upper
Mill Street (0259 52176).

Troon: Municipal Buildings, South
Beach (0292 317696).

Tyndrum: Invervey Hotel Car Park
(08384 246).

TRANSPORT

Comprehensive details of travel within south-west Scotland and the rest of the country are available from the **Travel Centre**, St Enoch Square, Glasgow (041–226 4826), which also offers full information on local buses and underground services in Glasgow itself.

Air

Glasgow Airport: Abbotsinch, Paisley (041–887 1111).

Port Ellen Airport: Isle of Islay (0496 2022). Flights to and from Glasgow Airport (30 minutes).

Prestwick Airport: Prestwick (0292 79822).

Bus

AA Buses: Boswell Park, Ayr (0292 263382). All towns between Troon and Stewarton.

MacEwan's Coach Services: Johnfield, Amisfield, Dumfries (0387 710357). Throughout Dumfries and Galloway, and to Edinburgh.

Midland Scottish: Stirling Bus Station, Goosecroft Road, Stirling (0786 73763). Excursions and regular services throughout the area.

Scottish Citylink: Head Office, Buchanan Bus Station, Killermont Street, Glasgow (041–332 9191). Network of services throughout Scotland.

Scottish Transport Group: Buchanan Street Bus Station, Glasgow (041–332 7133). Information on the Clydeside, Kelvin, Western and Eastern Scottish areas and bus groups.

Stagecoach and Cotters Coachline: Killermont Street, Glasgow (041–332 4100). Glasgow to London, Aberdeen and Inverness.

West Coast Motors: Campbeltown (0586 552319). Services covering Campbeltown and the Kintyre area, Inveraray, Oban and Mid Argyll.

Western Scottish Omnibus Ltd: Whitesands, Dumfries (0387 53496), and Sandgate, Ayr (0292 264623). Local and long-distance bus and coach services throughout south-west Scotland.

Ferry

Caledonian MacBrayne: The Ferry Terminal, Gourock (0475 33755). Clyde cruises and services around the Clyde, including Cowal, Bute, Arran, Islay, Gigha, Colonsay, Mull, Coll, Tiree, Skye and the Small Isles. 'Island Hopscotch' tickets available.

Clyde Marine Motoring Co Ltd: Princes Pier, Greenock (0475 21281). Kilcreggan to Gourock ferry services throughout the year (including Helensburgh, May–September).

Loch Lomond Sailings: Balloch Marina, Riverside, Balloch (0389 51481). Cruises on Loch Lomond.

Paddle Steamer *Waverley*: Anderston Quay, Glasgow (041–221 8152). Cruises around the Clyde River on the last sea-going paddle-steamer in the world.

P&O European Ferries Ltd: The Harbour, Cairnryan, near Stranraer (05812 276). Ferry crossings between Scotland and Ireland. Up to six sailings a day in each direction.

Sealink: Stranraer Harbour (0776 2262). Stranraer–Larne crossings and a number of excursions.

Western Ferries: Head Office, 16 Woodside Crescent, Glasgow (041–332 9766). Roll-on/Roll-off ferries between Port Askaig and Feolin.

Rail

Ayr (0292 284894).

Dumfries (0387 55115).

Girvan (0465 3369).

Glasgow (041–204 2844).

Greenock (0475 892247).

Irvine (0294 72111).

Kilmarnock (0563 41136).

Largs (0475 672178).

Lockerbie (057 62 2637).

Stirling (0786 64754).

Stranraer (0776 6234).

Gazetteer

ABERFOYLE
Central

On A81 3m E of Loch Ard.

Virtually equidistant from the **Lake of Menteith** and Loch Ard on the A81, Aberfoyle is a comfortable, well-heeled town on the edge of the Highlands, ideally situated as a base for day trips on foot. To the north, through Duke's Pass, lie the **Trossachs**; to the west, Queen Elizabeth National Forest Park, at the far end of which stands **Ben Lomond**, Scotland's southernmost Munro, or mountain over 3000 feet. The David Marshall Lodge visitor centre, just north of the town, provides parking, refreshments and maps for forest walks within the area. To the south-east, Doon Hill is an easy climb; the pine tree at its summit is said to house the ghost of a minister, Robert Kirk, spirited away from the material world for publishing a book, *The Secret Commonwealth* (1691), which gave details of local fairy legends.

AE
Dumfries and Galloway

Off A701 7½m N of Dumfries.

Best known as the shortest-named place in Scotland, this village is the starting point for two short forest walks.

AILSA CRAIG
Strathclyde

10m offshore from Girvan.

The rough midpoint in the sea between **Glasgow** and Belfast, the Craig, a volcanic plug two miles in circumference, was once host to banished monks, but is now a bird sanctuary. It is possible to visit the 1114-foot-high granite monolith by boat from **Girvan**.

AIRDRIE
Strathclyde

Off M8 12m E of Glasgow.

An ancient burgh, once a centre for light industry, Airdrie is now one of many commuter towns serving **Glasgow**, and is undergoing rapid redevelopment. The Weavers' Cottages, the oldest buildings in town, were recently demolished, and replaced by a museum devoted to the profession, which was once a mainstay of radical trade unionism in Scotland. Along with its largely Catholic neighbour **Coatbridge**, Airdrie is a reminder of the religious divisiveness which lingers on in west-central Scotland: Catholics and Protestants often concentrated themselves in separate towns or parts of towns. The Airdrie Savings Bank, with one branch in Airdrie and one in Coatbridge, is the only independent savings bank left in Britain.

ALLOA
Central

On A907 8m E of Stirling.

Now known mainly for its brewery, Alloa, before the River Forth silted up, was once one of the most important naval bases in Scotland. King James IV's ill-fated flagship, the *Great Michael* (a scale model

of which can be seen in the Royal
Scottish Museum, Edinburgh), was
launched from here in 1511.
Gartmorn Dam Country Park two
miles north-east includes the oldest
dam in Scotland.

ALLOWAY
Strathclyde

On A719 2m S of Ayr town centre.

The birthplace of **Robert Burns**,
Alloway is now a southern suburb
of **Ayr**, and can be reached in under
an hour on foot (via the main road,
the B7024) from the town centre.
The village is virtually given over
to a celebration of the poet, as
demonstrated by the fact that, on the
road out from Ayr, the signs saying
'Burns' are more prominent than
those saying Alloway. With four
separate sites within half a mile of
each other (**Alloway Kirkyard, Brig O'
Doon, Burns Cottage,** and the **Burns
Monument**), all of central significance
to his life and work, this is *the* place
to go for anyone with an interest in
Burns who lacks the time to visit the
myriad places scattered around the
south-west (such as **Souter Johnnie's
Cottage** in Kirkoswald, and Burns's
grave in **Dumfries**) which have some
connection with him. The **Land O'
Burns Centre** in Murdoch's Lone is a
visitor centre devoted to the poet.

ALLOWAY KIRKYARD
Alloway, Strathclyde

All year. Free.

Just across the road from the current
parish church stand the atmospheric
ruins of the old kirk where, in

the poem by **Robert Burns**, Tam O'
Shanter disturbed the witches in
their wild cavorting. Burns's father,
William Burnes, was buried here in
1784; his gravestone by the entrance
to the kirkyard also commemorates
the poet's mother, Agnes, *née*
Brown, who outlived her son and
was buried in Bolton churchyard,
East Lothian.

ALVA
Central

On A91 10m NE of Stirling.

A peaceful Hillfoots village, Alva
is dominated by the incongruously
large Strude Mill, built in 1828 and
once the centre of the area's woollen
industry. It is now converted
into flats. The picturesque,
waterfall-sprinkled Alva Glen to the
north of the village offers pleasant
hill-walking, although the descent is
steep and slippery in places.

ANNAN
Dumfries and Galloway

On A75 8m W of Gretna Green.

A small fishing town, Annan was
once the construction site of the
clippers which brought tea from
India. In less peaceful times, Annan
was the scene of fierce and frequent
fighting between Scots and English
soldiers: the resultant destruction
and rebuilding means that little of
antiquity survives. The most notable
relic is the Brus Stone, set into the
town hall, which comes from a
castle built by the noble family of
that name. It bears the name Robert
de Brus, believed to refer to King
Robert I.

The Antonine Wall

Built by the Romans in about AD 142, the Antonine Wall stretched from **Bo'ness** on the River Forth to Old Kilpatrick on the River **Clyde**, and was an expansion of the territory ostensibly under Roman control, superseding Hadrian's Wall to the south. Thirty-seven miles long, it was a turf rampart on stone foundations, with a ditch in front; the Romans knew from bitter experience that the inhabitants of the northern Lowlands were not the most peaceable people, and that they would come marauding southwards at any opportunity. Forts were placed at regular intervals along the wall, garrisoned by legionaries. As one author has written, 'of all the roads that led to Rome, one of the most unconvincing today must be the B816'; this is the road to Bonnybridge near which lies **Rough Castle**, the best preserved of these forts; its ramparts and ditches are still clearly visible. At **Bearsden** to the north-west of **Glasgow** there are the remains of a Roman bath-house, built for the use of the legionaries manning the wall.

Dr Lawrence Keppie of Glasgow's **Hunterian Museum**, where many artefacts from the wall are on display, has said that the Romans' stay in Scotland was 'rather like the Americans in Panama: a total waste of time'. Although we do not know the reason, that seems to have been the verdict of the Romans themselves, for they abandoned the wall only 20 years after it was built. Objects found along the wall are on display in the Hunterian, and include altars, crockery, weapons, distance slabs, and coins from the reign of the Emperor Antoninus Pius, after whom the wall was named. Glasgow's **Art Gallery and Museum**, Kelvingrove, also contains a distance slab, as well as models and replicas, while the Royal Scottish Museum in Edinburgh includes exhibits from the wall's eastern half.

ANTONINE WALL, see panel p71.

ARDCHATTAN PRIORY AND GARDENS
near Oban, Strathclyde

On N side of Lower Loch Etive, 6½ NE of Oban. Priory: all year. All reasonable times. Gardens: Apr-Nov, daily. D (P). Free. HS (031-244 3101).

Ardchattan Priory, founded in 1230, was the site of one of Robert the Bruce's parliaments, in 1308. The priory was burned by Cromwell's troops in 1654, the most significant surviving section being some carved stones.

ARDROSSAN
Strathclyde

On A78 8m S of Largs.

Contiguous to Saltcoats, but altogether more genteel, less hectically commercial, Ardrossan is the embarkation point for the ferry to Brodick, capital of the island of Arran. The ruins of the 12th-century Ardrossan Castle, destroyed by Oliver Cromwell's troops, overlook the bay; admission is free. There is good sea-fishing off the harbour.

ARDWELL HOUSE GARDENS
Ardwell, Dumfries and Galloway

On A716 11m SE of Stranraer. Mar-Oct, daily 1000-1800. D (P) (0776 2592).

The 18th-century Ardwell House itself is privately owned and not open to the public, but its gardens, which include some sub-tropical species, provide splendid views out into Luce Bay. For those with an interest in matters botanical, this is a worthwhile stop-off point on the road (the A716, then the B7065) to the Logan Botanic Gardens, three miles to the south.

ARGYLL WILDLIFE PARK
near Inveraray, Strathclyde

On A83 2m S of Inveraray on A83. All year. Daily 0930-1800 or dusk (0499 2264/2284).

A 55-acre site just off Loch Fyne, the park contains many Scottish species, such as wildcats and Soay sheep, as well as less familiar fauna – Père David's deer, Arctic and silver foxes, and a collection of rare owls. There is also a nature walk, and a woodland picnic area beside the loch. The gift shop and tearoom are closed in winter, when an honesty box operates for admission.

ARRAN
Strathclyde

Between Kintyre peninsula and Ayrshire coast.

Extremely busy during the summer holiday season, the island of Arran, 56 miles in circumference, is large enough, none the less, to accommodate those who prefer secluded hill-walking. The main route to Arran is by ferry from Ardrossan on the mainland to the capital, Brodick; those who cross by car can tour the whole island by the only main road, the A841, which follows the coastline for most of its way round. The economy of Arran is largely dependent on tourism, although sheep- and cattle-farming, as well as potatoes, are other sources of livelihood for the islanders. Three miles south of Brodick, looking out to **Holy Island**, is Lamlash, a small settlement best known for its annual angling competition. South again, by Whiting Bay, is the stone circle known as the Giant's Graves. The southern third of the island, indeed, boasts several sites of some antiquity, such as the Auchagallon stone circle and the Machrie standing stones. At Arran's northern end, Lochranza is the departure point for the summer ferry to Claonaig on the Kintyre peninsula. Now a ruin, Lochranza Castle is said to have been used by Robert the Bruce on his way back to the mainland to launch the decisive phase of the **Wars of Independence**. He is also said to have sheltered at King's Caves, by Blackwaterfoot in the south-west.

ARRAN, BRODICK CASTLE

Mid Apr–late Sept, daily 1300–1700; early Apr, first three weeks of Oct, Mon, Wed, Sat 1300–1700. Victorian and rhododendron gardens all year daily 0930–dusk. Restaurant and shop same dates as castle, but from 1000 and 1100 respectively. D (P). NTS (0770 2202).

Once the home of the Dukes of Hamilton, the castle now houses collections of silver, porcelain and paintings. It stands on a site which has long been used as a fortress; the oldest part of the current building is 13th century, with extensions having been added in the 17th century and the middle of the 19th.

ARRAN, GOATFELL

NTS.

The highest point on Arran (2866 feet), Goatfell offers rock-climbing, ridge-walking, and excellent views – although the most impressive sight on the isle is Goatfell itself, seen from below, when covered in snow. The National Trust for Scotland also owns part of neighbouring Glen Rosa and Cir Mhór.

AUCHENTOSHAN DISTILLERY
Duntocher, Strathclyde

Off A82 8m NW of Glasgow. All year. Mon–Fri from 0930, last tour 1530 (0389 79476).

Tours of the distillery, lasting around 45 minutes, explain the production process of the Auchentoshan single malt, which, unusually, is triple distilled. It is advisable to phone in advance.

AUCHINDRAIN
near Inveraray, Strathclyde

On A83 5½m SW of Inveraray. Easter–end Sept, daily 1000–1700 (closed Sat Apr, May, Sept). D (P) (04995 235).

This old west Highland township has been preserved, and in some places restored, to show the living and working conditions of ordinary Highlanders at various times in the past. Although the buildings themselves are simple cottages or sheds (and, in some cases, ruins), there is a certain austere grandeur about the whole place. To modern,

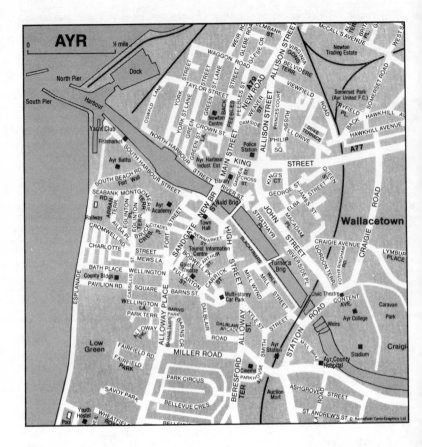

Town plan of Ayr

urban eyes, some of the buildings, such as the cottar's house, can seem closer to the Stone Age than to our own day, while the fact that there is only one sink in the township (in MacCallum's kitchen) gives some idea of how lacking almost all the inhabitants were in what would now be regarded as essential utilities. The visitor centre at the entrance to the township contains more displays and information about west Highland life.

AUCHINLECK BOSWELL MUSEUM
near Mauchline, Strathclyde

On A76 5m SE of Mauchline. Admission by arrangement: phone Mauchline Tourist Information (0290 51916) for details.

James Boswell (1740–95), man of letters and biographer of Samuel Johnson, set out from here with the doctor on their tour of the Highlands in 1773, and is buried here along with four other generations of his family. The museum stands alongside the family tomb.

AYR
Strathclyde

On A78 3m S of Prestwick.

The heart of Burns country, with the town centre only a couple of miles from the poet's birthplace in **Alloway**, and within striking distance of places of significance to the poet such as **Mauchline, Souter Johnnie's Cottage** in Kirkoswald, and the **Bachelors' Club** in Tarbolton, Ayr, the largest town on the Firth of **Clyde**, also caters well for the less

poetically minded. Golf is the great sporting attraction in the area, with a particularly fine public course, the Belleisle, in Belleisle Park; Ayr Racecourse, on Whitletts Road, is the site of the annual Scottish Grand National horse race; and there are, in general, good leisure facilities for families. The Wonderwest World holiday centre and fun park lies just outside the town.

In Burns Statue Square in the town centre, the statue of the poet stands on a traffic island, gazing southwards to Alloway. There is nothing to detain the visitor on the road to Alloway until, half a mile before the village, you come to **Rozelle Park**. Back in the heart of Ayr, the Auld Kirk, just off the High Street, is where Burns was baptized. It is generally thought that the bard 'sometimes' attended church here. The attractive Auld Brig, the original, medieval road over the River Ayr, was substantially restored early this century to allow it to take motor traffic; River Street runs from it to the New Bridge, a 19th-century replacement for the first 'new' bridge which, as Burns predicted in the poem 'The Brigs of Ayr', was outlasted by the old one.

Just north of the New Bridge, on a traffic island in Main Street, stands Newton Steeple which, erected in 1795, stood atop the council chambers of the then-independent burgh, Newton-on-Ayr. The chambers were demolished in the 1960s, when the steeple was preserved and removed to its present position. St John's Tower, off Cromwell Road, is all that remains of the old burgh kirk of St John the Baptist where, in April 1315, almost a year after the Battle of **Bannockburn**, the Scottish parliament met to confirm the succession of the crown. St John's having been commandeered to form part of Oliver Cromwell's citadel, the town was paid compensation to help towards the building of the replacement, the Auld Kirk. Wallace Tower, in the High Street, houses a statue of Sir William Wallace by James Thom, the local man who also sculpted the statues of Tam O' Shanter and friends at the **Burns Monument** in Alloway. **Loudoun Hall**, also in the town, can be visited. The ruined **Dunure Castle** lies six miles to the south-west of Ayr.

AYR, LOUDOUN HALL

In Boat Vennel. Jul–Aug, Mon–Sat 1100–1600 or by arrangement. D (P). Free (0292 282109/611290).

Loudoun Hall is a fine town house of the early 16th century, one of the few surviving examples of such in Scotland.

BACHELORS' CLUB
Tarbolton, Strathclyde

On B744 in Tarbolton 7½m NE of Ayr.
Apr–Oct, daily 1200–1700. D (P) NTS
(0292 541940).

The Bachelors' Club is a 17th-century thatched house where poet **Robert Burns** and his friends formed a debating society in 1780. Burns was initiated into freemasonry in the club the following year. The house contains period furnishings.

BALLANTRAE
Strathclyde

On A77 13m SW of Girvan.

A small village on the mouth of the River Stinchar, Ballantrae gave its name to Robert Louis Stevenson's novel *The Master of Ballantrae*, the setting for which is in fact further south. The churchyard of the village's present place of worship contains the Kennedy Aisle, the only remaining section of the old kirk, built in the early years of the 17th century as a memorial to Gilbert Kennedy of Bargany, killed at **Maybole** by his kinsman, the Earl of Cassillis. Ardstinchar Castle, also a ruin, was home to the Bargany branch of the Kennedys, for a long time one of the most powerful families in the area.

BALLOCH
Strathclyde

Off A82 at S end of Loch Lomond.

Its position at the southern end of **Loch Lomond** and the frequent train service from **Glasgow** make Balloch more of a staging-post than a destination in its own right, although it is the main centre for visitors to the loch. Passenger boats leave from here en route to some of the loch's islands (including **Bucinch and Ceardach**) and the lochside towns further north, while the more adventurous can hire small craft for themselves. Just to the north is Balloch Castle Country Park and visitor centre, 200 acres of parkland, woodland and gardens sloping gently down to the loch.

BALQUHIDDER
Central

Off A84 12m NW of Callander.

At the eastern end of Loch Voil, and on the northern edge of the **Trossachs**, Balquhidder is where **Rob Roy Macgregor** (1671–1734) lived, died and was buried. For some Scotland's answer to Robin Hood, Rob Roy was regarded by others as a common thief of an uncommonly violent disposition. He did, however, die peacefully in his own house in the village, and was interred in the village kirkyard; his wife and two of their sons are buried alongside him. The Rob Roy Tryst and Clan Gregor Heritage Centre two miles east of the village sell handicrafts, books and gift items. The Rob Roy and Trossachs Visitor Centre in **Callander** gives more information on the man and his life, while Sir Walter Scott's novel *Rob Roy* paints a colourful if typically prolix picture.

BANNOCKBURN HERITAGE CENTRE
near Stirling, Central

Off A9 2m S of Stirling. Late Mar–late Oct, daily 1000–1800. Site of battle open all year. D. NTS (0786 812664).

Just off Bannockburn village's main road, the centre commemorates the Battle of Bannockburn in 1314, the climax of the **Wars of Independence** against England, and the greatest military victory in Scotland's history. Displays explain the events leading up to Bannockburn, such as the Battle of Stirling Bridge (1397), culminating in a huge mural of the battle itself. The mural merits careful scrutiny: it gives a realistic idea of the claustrophobic crush there must have been, and of the fate suffered by the defeated. The centre also includes the Kingdom of the Scots exhibition, portraying the country's major figures up to King James VI and the Union of the Crowns, setting Bannockburn in its historical context. The audio-visual presentation, lasting 15 minutes, gives a concise and lucid explanation of how King Robert the Bruce, in under a decade, made the transition from virtually friendless fugitive to liberator of his land and people. Outside the centre, a rotunda encloses the Borestone site which is said to have been Bruce's command post during the battle. An equestrian statue of the king stands nearby, while the battle itself was fought on the open fields down towards the burn.

BARNWEIL CHURCH AND TOWER
near Symington, Strathclyde

Of A77 8m NE of Ayr. Open by arrangement with Kyle and Carrick District Council.

The church, not used since 1673, is now a ruin; the tower, built in 1855, commemorates William Wallace.

BEARSDEN
Strathclyde

A salubrious northern suburb of **Glasgow**, Bearsden was the site of a small Roman settlement, one of many dotted along the **Antonine Wall** in the second century AD. While several of the significant finds have been removed to **Glasgow's Hunterian Museum**, the remains of a bath-house may still be seen by the Roman road.

BEN LOMOND
Strathclyde

By Rowardennan on eastern shore of Loch Lomond. NTS.

The southernmost Munro, or Scottish mountain over 3000 feet, Ben Lomond is one of the best known and most popular mountains in the country. It is both easy to get to and then not too arduous a climb, with a path leading to the summit, from where, in clear weather, there are superlative views down the loch. The site of over 5000 acres also includes Beinn Uird, Ptarmigan and Sron Aonaich.

BENNANE HEAD
Strathclyde

On A77 8m SW of Girvan.

The lay-by on the Bennane Head clifftop is a welcome place to stop in clement weather, with views out to **Ailsa Craig** and beyond. On the shore below, accessible with care, is a less pleasant spot, Sawney Beane's Cave, the reputed home of the 17th-century cannibal and his family, who disposed of a number of travellers before being captured and executed.

BIGGAR
Strathclyde

On A702 10m SW of Lanark.

On the far eastern edge of Strathclyde, Biggar is a small, well-preserved market town. The church, still in use, in Kirkstyle, was built in 1545 by Malcolm, Lord Fleming of Biggar, the uncle of Mary Queen of Scots. Biggar Puppet Theatre, just east of the town on the B7016, is a complete Victorian miniature theatre, with exhibitions and guided tours. **Biggar Gasworks Museum** can be visited.

BIGGAR GASWORKS MUSEUM
Biggar, Strathclyde

Gasworks Road (near the war memorial). Contact the National Museums of Scotland (031–225 7534).

An unusual but interesting place to visit, being Britain's oldest surviving rural gasworks, built in 1839. Decommissioned in 1973, it is the only coal-gas station in Scotland; much of the machinery is still in working order, and guided tours are available.

BLACKHILL
Strathclyde

Off B7018 3m W of Lanark. All year. Free. NTS.

A five-acre site, Blackhill is a good vantage point for viewing the Clyde valley, and contains a cairn and an Iron Age hill fort.

BLAIR DRUMMOND SAFARI PARK
near Stirling, Central

Off A84 6m W of Stirling. Late Mar–early Oct, daily 1000–1630. D (P) (0786 841456).

The only safari park in Scotland, Blair Drummond houses big cats, elephants, chimps and sea-lions among many other species. There are drive-through reserves, and boat journeys round Chimpanzee Island and the bird sanctuary. The pets' farm, an adventure playground, a resident clown and refreshment facilities ensure an active day out for families. Needless to say, as the park houses wild animals, the instructions of the staff must be heeded, and the greatest of care should be taken while driving through.

BLAIRLOGIE
Central

Off A91 2m NE of Stirling.

Peaceful and picturesque, Blairlogie is the westernmost village in the Hillfoots, the group of small communities which includes **Menstrie** (less than two miles further east), **Tillicoultry** and **Alva**. The castle which looms over the village is closed to the public. Nearby, close to the Logie Burn, stands the ruined Logie Old Kirk, dating from around 1684.

BO'NESS
Central

Off M9 12 m NW of Edinburgh.

A pleasant, orderly town beside the Firth of Forth, Bo'ness and its traditional stone houses are becoming increasingly popular as a commuting base for Edinburgh. Its slightly old-fashioned, sleepy feel belies its past. Bo'ness (a contraction of Borrowstounness) was once a busy industrial town and port. Here James Watt experimented in 1764 with his steam engine on the Kinneil Estate. Henry Bell, who launched an early steam boat on the River Clyde in 1812, is also associated with Bo'ness. Local attractions include the **Bo'ness and Kinneil Railway**.

BO'NESS AND KINNEIL RAILWAY
Bo'ness, Central

Off Union Street, Bo'ness. Sat–Sun (0506 822298).

At the edge of the Firth of Forth to the east of **Bo'ness** is a railway station from where, at weekends, steam trains run to Kinneil. Shiny locomotives, of enduring appeal, pull historic rolling stock the short distance before returning for another load of passengers. Enthusiasts linger around the station all day, looking wistfully at the train drivers and engineers.

BOTHWELL CASTLE
Uddingston, Strathclyde

Off A74 7m SE of Glasgow. Apr–Sept, Mon–Sat 0930–1900, Sun 1400–1900; Oct–Mar, Sat, Mon–Wed 0930–1600, Thurs 0930–1200, Sun 1400–1600 (0698 816894).

Originally constructed in the 13th century, Bothwell Castle was rebuilt two centuries later by the Douglas family. Still one of the most impressive stone castles in the country, it holds a commanding position above the Clyde valley. The Battle of Bothwell Brig took place nearby in 1679, a body of Covenanters being routed by a royalist force under the command of Monmouth, the illegitimate son of King Charles II.

BREADALBANE
Central

North of the **Trossachs**, the Breadalbane area, originally an estate owned by the earls of that name, constitutes the most northerly section of Central Region, and stretches into Tayside. **Crianlarich** and **Tyndrum** to the west, and **Killin** to the east, are the largest communities. The Rivers Lochay and Dochart run through Breadalbane, and the Falls of Dochart, at Killin, make for an impressive end to a day's walking through the area.

BRIDGE OF ALLAN
Central

On A9 2m N of Stirling.

A small, prosperous commuter town, with many residents working in **Glasgow** or Edinburgh as well as **Stirling** itself, Bridge of Allan was once popular with holidaymakers as a spa resort. The town is the starting point for some short, undemanding

Robert Burns

Scotland's national poet, Robert Burns (1759–96) was born in **Alloway**, near **Ayr**, on 25 January, the son of a farmer, William Burnes. Robert himself attempted to make a go of farming, but failed and was impoverished for most of his life. In 1786, his decision to emigrate to Jamaica was reversed at the last minute by the publication of the **Kilmarnock** edition of his poems; it was a great success, and Burns became the toast of Edinburgh literary society. That same year he enjoyed his celebrated flirtatious correspondence with 'Clarinda', as he called Agnes Maclehose; the previous year, he had an affair with 'Highland Mary'. For all his occasional infidelities to her, Jean Armour appears to have been the most important woman in his life, and he married her in 1788. He leased **Ellisland** farm near **Dumfries** in the year of his marriage, but was almost immediately in difficulties with it. He became an exciseman in 1789, ensuring himself of some income, and, when the farm failed in 1790, he moved to Dumfries. He suffered from rheumatism in his later years, an ailment which reputedly contributed to his death.

Burns's unwaning popularity, which is strong in many other countries as well as in Scotland, is based partly on the songs he contributed to James Johnson's *Scots Musical Museum*, and partly on triumphs such as 'Tam O' Shanter' (written in one day). This remains the best long narrative poem in Scots, while among the most accomplished of Burns's shorter works are 'Holy Willie's Prayer' (a masterful exposé of hypocrisy), 'To A Mouse', and 'To The Haggis'. Monuments to him are dotted along the Burns Trail, a visitor route which includes the cottage where he was born. His birthday is celebrated with Burns Suppers all over the world.

walks along the River Allan, and to **Dunblane**, via the Darn Road Walk, a distance of about two miles. The entrance to Stirling University campus is at the Stirling end of town.

BRIG O' DOON
Alloway, Strathclyde

All year. D.

This single-arch span, high above the river, is famed as the escape route taken by Tam O' Shanter, hero of the **Robert Burns** poem of the same name, as he fled the witches, who, unable to cross water, could follow no further. Built in the 13th century, it is an attractive, cobbled public right of way.

BRUCE'S STONE
Dumfries and Galloway

By A712 6m W of New Galloway. All year. D. Free. NTS (041–552 8391).

A granite boulder on Moss Raploch marks the spot of Scotland's King Robert the Bruce's first victory over the English in the **Wars of Independence**.

BRUCE'S STONE
Dumfries and Galloway

Off A714 13m W of Newton Stewart. All year. Free (0671 2431).

At under ten miles away from its namesake west of **New Galloway**, this is also a granite memorial to King Robert's victory in 1307 over the English. It stands on the north side of Loch Trool at the

bottom of the Merrick, southern Scotland's highest hill (as opposed to mountain).

BUCINCH AND CEARDACH
Loch Lomond, Strathclyde

In Loch Lomond between Luss and Balmaha. All year. Free. NTS.

These two small islands in **Loch Lomond**, neither of them inhabited, can be reached quite easily in reasonable weather by boat.

ROBERT BURNS, see panel p81.

ROBERT BURNS CENTRE
Dumfries, Dumfries and Galloway

Mill Road, Dumfries. Apr–Sept, Mon–Sat 1000–2000, Sun 1400–1700; Oct–Mar, Tue–Sat 1000–1300, 1400–1700. D. Free (0387 64808).

The central feature of the Robert Burns heritage trail which runs through Dumfries and Galloway, the Robert Burns Centre is housed in a sandstone mill on the banks of the River Nith. There is an audio-visual presentation, an exhibition on the life of the poet in **Dumfries**, a bookshop and a café.

BURNS COTTAGE AND MUSEUM
Alloway, Strathclyde

All year. Jun–Aug, daily 0900–1900; Apr, May, Sept, Oct, Mon–Sat 1000–1700, Sun 1400–1700; Nov–Mar, Mon–Sat 1000–1600.

D. Admission charge also permits entry to **Burns Monument and Gardens** *(0292 41215).*

Built by his father, William Burnes, this white, thatched cottage was where Scotland's national poet Robert Burns was born on 25 January 1759, a date still commemorated by Scots and Burns enthusiasts around the world. A simple family dwelling, which would have been shared by farm animals, it was restored to its original state after being acquired by the Burns Monument Trustees in 1880. It contains functional period furniture and agricultural implements. In a corner of the front room stands the cubby hole bed where Burns was born. The museum contains original manuscripts and letters, and is a useful introduction to Burns. A wallchart places him in context both historically, by documenting the main events of the time such as the French Revolution, and artistically, listing the births and deaths of those writers – Robert Fergusson, for instance – who influenced his development. The main stages of Burns's own life are also documented, with illustrations and apposite quotations from his works.

BURNS MONUMENT AND GARDENS
Alloway, Strathclyde

All year. Jun–Aug, daily 0900–1900; Apr, May, Sept, Oct, Mon–Sat 1000–1700, Sun 1400–1700; Nov–Mar, Mon–Sat 1000–1600. D (P). Admission charge also permits entry to **Burns Cottage and Museum** *(0292 41321).*

Planned in 1814 and opened in 1823, the monument to Scotland's national poet looks like the type of small Greek temple devoted to a single deity – a fitting comparison, given the reverence in which so many people have held the poet. The ground floor contains memorabilia, and a display of foreign-language editions of his work, while, a floor up, a narrow walkway allows a view of the **Brig O' Doon**. In a separate building in the gardens stand the impressive stone figures of characters from Burns's poems: Tam O' Shanter, his drinking crony Souter Johnnie, and the cheery landlady Nanse Tunnock. Carved by James Thom and presented to the monument the year after it opened, the statues are, like the tales of Tam himself, slightly larger than life. These ones are kept inside for protection from the elements, but copies can be seen outside in the garden of **Souter Johnnie's Cottage** in Kirkoswald.

BURNSWARK
near Ecclefechan, Dumfries and Galloway

1½m N of B725. All year. Free (057 65 203).

Also known as Birrenswark, after the remains of the Birrens fort, the site contains a Roman artillery range and a Scots or Pictish hill fort. The proximity of the two has led to the assumption that the hill fort may have been artificially constructed by the Romans for use in close-combat training.

BUTE, ISLE OF
Strathclyde

Off southern end of Cowal peninsula.

Only 10 minutes by ferry from Colintraive in Argyll, and half an hour from Wemyss Bay, the island of Bute – particularly its capital, Rothesay – is still a popular holiday destination for west-of-Scotland city-dwellers. Golf and watersports, ceilidhs and cruises cater for the island's traditional clientèle, while the north-western quarter is fine, unspoilt walking territory.

BUTE, ARDENCRAIG GARDENS

Early May–late Sept, Mon–Fri 0900–1630, Sat–Sun 1300–1630. D (P). Free (0700 4225).

At Ardencraig just south of Rothesay, the gardens produce plants for displays throughout the island, and include aviaries and fish ponds.

BUTE, ROTHESAY CASTLE

Apr–Sept, Mon–Sat 0930–1900, Sun 1400–1900; Oct–Mar, Sat, Mon–Wed 0930–1600, Thurs 1300–1600, Sun 1400–1600. D (P). HS (031–244 3101).

Rothesay Castle was built at the turn of the 11th century, and has seen many violent disputes over control of it, from the Battle of **Largs** in 1265 to the Monmouth Rebellion 420 years later. Burned during the latter event, it was restored in the 19th century.

CAERLAVEROCK CASTLE AND NATURE RESERVE
near Dumfries, Dumfries and Galloway

Off B725 9m S of Dumfries. Castle: Apr–Sept, Mon–Sat 0930–1900, Sun 1400–1900; Oct–Mar, Mon–Sat 0930–1600, Sun 1400–1600. Nature reserve: all year. D (P). Free.

Built in the 13th century, the triangular-shaped Caerlaverock Castle was for a long time a stronghold of the Maxwell family, its position in marshland a boon to defenders. Damaged in sieges by the Covenanters and earlier by Edward I of England, and abandoned by the Maxwells in the late 17th century, its dilapidated state only augments its air of romantic austerity. Near to the castle, the reserve run by the Nature Conservancy Council is a 14 000-acre saltmarsh site. The 600-acre sanctuary within it, access to which is restricted, includes many threatened species of birds, and a now-thriving colony of natterjack toads.

CALLANDER
Central

On A84 15m NW of Stirling.

A tourist town since Victorian times, Callander is the largest community in the **Trossachs**. The Rob Roy and Trossachs Visitor Centre, in Ancaster Square, has an audio-visual presentation and displays about the famous outlaw, who lived and died in **Balquhidder**, to the north. Just south-west of Callander on the A84 to **Doune** is the Heather Centre and Miniature Railway, a combination

of activities for adults and children, with garden displays and more than 100 varieties of heather for the former, and adventure playgrounds as well as the miniature railway for younger visitors. Callander Crags just to the north, more accessible than they may at first appear, provide good views in all directions: the best vantage point is the Queen Victoria Jubilee Cairn, looking northwards to Ben Vorlich, and south-east to **Stirling**, the Ochils, and even the Pentland Hills on the outskirts of Edinburgh.

CAMPBELTOWN
Kintyre peninsula, Strathclyde

On Kintyre peninsula, on A83 5m E of Machrihanish.

Standing at the head of its eponymous loch, Campbeltown, once a fishing port, now offers more leisurely sailing to the holidaymakers who are essential to its economy. It is surprisingly busy considering its remote position on the Kintyre peninsula, and has a small industrial estate and an airport. Prosperous and well kept, it is in a picturesque setting on the edge of the horseshoe-shaped loch. The island of Davaar, at the mouth of Campbeltown Loch, is accessible at low tide. It was once inhabited, but now only sheep live there.

CANONBIE
Dumfries and Galloway

Off A7 2m N of Border.

An area between the Rivers Esk and Sark, Canonbie was known in the Middle Ages as the Debatable Land, as it was a lawless location not properly under the control of either the Scots or the English authorities. **Gilnockie Tower** in Canonbie was home to the most renowned Borders reiver, or cattle thief, Johnnie Armstrong. The hanging of Armstrong and his colleagues in 1530, and the building of Scots Dyke in 1552 to form the agreed border, brought an end to the anarchy.

CARFIN
Strathclyde

On A723 3m NE of Motherwell.

Otherwise an unremarkable village, Carfin is the site of a grotto, dedicated in 1922 to Our Lady of Lourdes. Since then, it has attracted a sizeable number of Roman Catholic pilgrims.

CARLETON CASTLE
near Girvan, Strathclyde

Off A77 6m S of Girvan. All year. Free.

A now-ruined watch-tower, built by the Kennedy family, the castle was the home, according to a ballad, of a baron who pushed seven rich wives off the cliff, but then suffered the same fate at the hands of his altogether cannier eighth wife.

CARRICK CASTLE
near Lochgoilhead, Strathclyde

Off B839 5m S of Lochgoilhead. All year. D. Free.

Burned by the Earl of Atholl's forces in 1685, the castle dates from the

14th century and, the lack of a roof notwithstanding, has weathered the centuries well. Privately owned, it may be viewed from the outside only.

CARRICK FOREST
near Girvan, Strathclyde

8m SE of Girvan.

Walks through the forest, some signposted, head north towards Straiton and east to Loch Doon, which forms the boundary with Dumfries and Galloway. The ruined Loch Doon Castle on the south-west shore was moved to its present site from an island in the loch when the water level was raised. It was once the home of John Balliol, the ineffectual king who ruled Scotland briefly at the end of the 13th century before Robert the Bruce began his struggle to unify the realm and end English domination.

CASSILLIS HOUSE
near Maybole, Strathclyde

Off B742 4m NE of Maybole.

Built and still owned by the Kennedy family, the house, which may be viewed only from the outside, dates from the 14th century.

CASTLE CAMPBELL
Central

In Dollar Glen, off A91 1m N of Dollar. Late Mar–late Sept, Mon–Sat 0930–1900,

Sun 1400–1900; early Oct–late Mar,
Mon–Wed, Sat 0930–1600, Thurs
0930–1300, Sun 1400–1600. NTS
(031–244 3101).

Once the home of the chief of Clan
Campbell, the castle dates from the
end of the 15th century. Its position
in a clearing in **Dollar** Glen offers
good views of the Forth valley.
Dollar Glen itself is an excellent
venue for peaceful woodland walks,
its steep paths going across narrow
bridges and through beautiful
scenery, including waterfalls.

CASTLE DOUGLAS
Dumfries and Galloway

Off A75 9m NE of Kirkcudbright.

Formerly known as Carlingwark
– it stands just by the loch of that
name – the market town of Castle
Douglas, the site of a human
settlement since the Iron Age, was
renamed two centuries ago after
William Douglas, who returned, a
rich man, from the Americas and
transformed the town's economy.
Threave Castle and **Threave Gardens**
are nearby.

CASTLE KENNEDY GARDENS
near Stranraer, Dumfries and
Galloway

Off A75 3m E of Stranraer. Apr–Sept, daily
1000–1700. D (0776 2024).

These fine botanical gardens,
including a long monkey-puzzle
avenue, were begun in the early
18th century. Castle Kennedy itself
was burned down in 1715, and

the ruins now blend in well with
the flora.

CASTLE STALKER
Strathclyde

Off Port Appin, 25m NE of Oban. Open by
appointment Mar–Sept (088 362 2768).

Standing on a tiny island in Loch
Linnhe, the recently restored castle
was built by the Stewarts of Appin
at the start of the 16th century.
Its situation, and simplicity of
style, endow it with an appealing
austerity.

CHATELHERAULT LODGE
near Hamilton, Strathclyde

At Ferniegair, off A72 1½m S of
Hamilton. House: all year, daily 1100–1600.
Visitor centre: early Apr–late Sept, daily
1030–1800; early Oct–late Mar, daily
1030–1700. D (P) (0698 426213).

Built by William Adam in 1732 for
the Duke of Hamilton, the hunting
lodge and kennels have been
restored, and along with the visitor
centre, provide an informative
picture of antique affluence. The
surrounding country park includes
woodland walks, a children's play
area, an Iron Age fort, and a herd of
white cattle.

CLACHAN BRIDGE
near Oban, Strathclyde

Off B844 12m SW of Oban. All times. D.
Free (0631 63122).

Said to be the only bridge that spans the Atlantic, Clachan Bridge crosses Seil Sound, linking the mainland with Seil Island. A single-arched bridge, it was built in 1792.

RIVER CLYDE, see panel p145.

CLYDEBANK
Strathclyde

On A82 8m NW of Glasgow city centre.

Heavily bombed during the Blitz of World War II, Clydebank, now a rather characterless suburb of Glasgow, was once part of a vast shipping industry on the Clyde. The *Queen Mary* was launched, from John Brown's yard, in 1934; the *Queen Elizabeth* four years later; and Britain's last-ever battleship, HMS *Vanguard*, was launched in 1944. The town is now best known as the home of a ten-screen cinema and the local, independent radio station Radio Clyde.

COATBRIDGE
Strathclyde

Off M8 9m E of Glasgow city centre.

In Monklands District east of Glasgow Coatbridge is the Catholic mirror of Protestant Airdrie, a model, like its neighbour, of high unemployment and urban blight. The Summerlee Heritage Trust in West Canal Street is an award-winning museum of industrial and social history.

COLL, ISLE OF
Strathclyde

Off NW coast of Mull.

The northernmost island in Strathclyde, Coll and its southerly neighbour Tiree lie west of Mull. About 12 miles long and four miles wide, Coll once had a thriving population of crofters. In the middle of the last century, the factor to the Duke of Argyll put rents up to a level such that many islanders had to emigrate to Canada, no longer able to afford to stay in their birthplace. The island's economy today still depends partially on farming, as well as on tourism and commercial fishing. Visitors fishing for pleasure rather than commercial gain will find ample stocks of trout in Coll's lochs. Although the eastern coastline is rocky, the western seaboard has some sandy bays which are good spots for bathing. Arinagour, a village of white-washed cottages, is the main population centre; the island has little more than 100 'full-time' inhabitants, but second-home owners and tourists augment that number considerably in season.

COLONSAY AND ORONSAY
Strathclyde

10m W of Jura.

The ferry which departs from Oban is the easiest and most regular route to Colonsay, an unspoilt, sparsely populated island eight miles long by two miles wide, with a wealth of flora and fauna, and a surprisingly mild climate. Scalasaig is the largest settlement on the island, rather unattractive in itself, although the path behind the hotel there takes the walker to the Vale of Kiloran, a beautiful hilly stretch of fields and woods. Oronsay, the southern and smaller of the two islands, is accessible from Colonsay at low tide. The two are named after St Columba and St Oran, who stopped off here en route from Ireland to Iona; St Oran's Chapel on Oronsay is an impressively stark 14th-century ruin.

CRAIGCLEUCH COLLECTION
near Langholm, Dumfries and Galloway

On B709 2m NW of Langholm. Easter, early May–late Sept, daily 1000–1700 or by arrangement. D. (P) (03873 80137).

A collection of rare ethnographical artefacts from around the world – from African carvings to Chinese jade animals – is housed in a 19th-century Scots baronial mansion. There are woodland walks around the house.

CRAIGNETHAN CASTLE
near Lanark, Strathclyde

Off A72 5m NW of Lanark. Apr–Sept, Mon–Sat 0930–1900, Sun 1400–1900; Oct–Mar, Mon–Sat 0930–1600, Sun 1400–1600. HS (031–244 3101).

Owned by the Hamilton family, supporters of Mary Queen of Scots, the castle came under constant attack after the latter's fall, and was partially destroyed in 1579. Well preserved despite these depredations, Craignethan was designed as a stronghold rather than a peaceful country retreat, and includes the earliest known example

in Britain of a *caponier* – a concealed passageway designed to house gunners defending the castle.

CRARAE GARDEN
Strathclyde

Near Minard, on A83 10m S of Inveraray. Daily, summer 0900–1800; winter daylight hours. Visitor centre, Easter–Oct 1000–1700. D (P) (0546 86614/86607).

On the west shore of Loch Fyne, Crarae is especially noted for azaleas, eucalyptus and rhododendrons. The woodland garden, set in a glen, contains a number of waterfalls.

CREETOWN GEMROCK MUSEUM
near Gatehouse of Fleet, Dumfries and Galloway

Chain Road, Creetown, off A75 11m W of Gatehouse of Fleet. Daily, Easter–Sept 0930–1800; Oct–Easter 0930–1700. D (0671 82 357/554).

A collection of gems and minerals from all over the world, the Creetown Gemrock Museum houses one of the biggest collections of minerals in Britain, and includes examples of almost every known gemstone and mineral. A lapidary workshop shows how the museum's exhibits are made ready for display, and a crystal cave displays many of the exhibits to their best advantage.

CRIANLARICH
Central

On A85 11m SW of Killin.

A village on the main rail route south to **Glasgow**, Crianlarich is just off the **West Highland Way**, and is a popular, picturesque stopping-off point for walkers.

CRINAN CANAL
Strathclyde

On A83 2m SW of Ardrishaig.

Constructed in the 18th century, Crinan Canal connects Loch Fyne, at Ardrishaig, with the Sound of Jura, at Crinan. Just nine miles long, it saves a journey round the Kintyre peninsula of 130 miles; this was once a great boon to the fishing fleets, although the canal is now used chiefly as a leisure waterway.

CROSSRAGUEL ABBEY
near Maybole, Strathclyde

On A77 2m SW of Maybole. Apr–Sept, Mon–Sat 0930–1900, Sun 1400–1900; Oct–Mar, Mon, Tues, Wed, Sat 0930–1600, Sun 1400–1600. D (P). HS (031–244 3101).

A Benedictine monastery from its foundation in 1244 until the end of the 16th century, Crossraguel, now a ruin, is an example of ecclesiastic architecture of the period.

CRUACHAN PUMPED STORAGE POWER STATION
Central

Off A85 18m E of Oban. Easter-Oct, daily 0900–1630. D (P) (086 62 673).

A seemingly unlikely site of interest, Cruachan power station is built into the heart of the mountain.

Because of this, it is almost entirely concealed from view. Secluded in a beautiful, bleak setting 1200 feet up Ben Cruachan, the power station uses water pumped up from Loch Awe. There is a visitor centre, and a guided minibus tour which takes you deep into the mountain.

CULZEAN CASTLE AND COUNTRY PARK
nearMaybole, Strathclyde

On A719 4m W of Maybole. Early Apr–late Oct, daily 1030–1730. Country Park, all year, daily 0930–sunset. D (P). NTS (065 56 269).

Culzean Castle, built from 1772 to 1792, is one of Robert Adam's most famous works, and the most visited of all the National Trust for Scotland's properties. Constructed on a clifftop, around an ancient stronghold of the Kennedy family, Culzean was originally the home of the Earl of Cassillis. The whole building is sumptuously appointed, especially noteworthy being the round drawing room and the oval staircase. The Eisenhower Room explains the career of the United States' soldier-president and his links with Culzean. One of the conditions when the 5th Marquess of Ailsa and the Kennedy family gave the castle to the National Trust was that a room be set aside for anyone whom Scotland might want to honour: in the aftermath of World War II, Eisenhower, who had been supreme commander of the Allies' D-Day forces, was an appropriate choice. The country park, Scotland's first, was opened in 1970; at their best in spring, summer and autumn, its 563 acres contain woodland walks, an adventure playground for children, a deer park and a swan pond.

CUMBERNAULD
Strathclyde

Off A80 10m N of Airdrie.

Close to the border with Central Region, Cumbernauld was established as a New Town just after World War II to house the Glasgow overspill, although there has been a settlement on the site since Roman times – the **Antonine Wall** lies just to the north. Two and a half miles south-east of Cumbernauld, Palacerigg Country Park of the town) is home to wild cats, wolves and other wildlife, and also has pony-trekking and nature trails.

CUMBRAE
Strathclyde

Car and passenger ferry from Largs.

Only a few minutes by ferry from **Largs**, the islands of Great and Little Cumbrae – especially Millport on the former – are popular day-trip

and holiday destinations for west-coast town-dwellers, especially those with an interest in watersports. Little Cumbrae is easily accessible by boat from Millport. Funding for Millport pier will soon enable larger boats to berth there; it is hoped that this will attract back some of the custom which was lost when foreign holidays became more affordable. The Cathedral of the Isles in Millport is said to be the smallest cathedral in Europe.

CUNNINGHAME GRAHAM MEMORIAL
near Aberfoyle, Central

Gartmore, off A81 2½m SW of Aberfoyle. All year. NTS.

A memorial cairn to the Scots author, politician and adventurer R. B. (Robert Bontine) Cunninghame Graham (1852–1936), the first president of both the Scottish Labour Party and the Scottish National Party. The cairn originally stood at Castlehill in Dumbarton, and was moved to its present site in 1981.

DALGARVEN MILL
Kilwinning, Strathclyde

On A737, Dalry Road, Kilwinning.
All year. Mon–Sat 1000–1700. D (P)
(0294 52448).

Housed in a restored water mill
which dates from the beginning
of the 17th century, Dalgarven
Mill is an agricultural and costume
museum, with changing displays
of local life and clothing of
centuries past.

DEAN CASTLE
Kilmarnock, Strathclyde

Dean Road, off Glasgow Road, Kilmarnock.
All year. Daily 1200–1700. D (P)
(0536 22702/26401).

Set in a 200-acre country park,
the ancestral home of the Boyd
family dates from the 14th and 15th
centuries, and contains a diverse
range of exhibits, from medieval
weaponry to manuscripts of
Robert Burns.

DEVIL'S BEEF TUB
Dumfries and Galloway

On A701 6m N of Moffat. D. Free
(0683 20620).

Easily seen from the road, the
Devil's Beef Tub is a natural hollow
among the hills, and is the source
of the River Annan. Frequently
shrouded in mist, it was used up
until the 18th century by cattle
thieves (or reivers) as the perfect
place to hide their catch.

DOLLAR
Central

On A91 12m W of Stirling.

The most easterly and affluent of
the Hillfoots villages, Dollar is best
known for its Academy, a private
school which accounts for a third of
the population. The Academy was
founded with a large bequest from
John Macnab, a native of Dollar who
made his fortune in London. Dollar
Glen, a wooded, 60-acre site owned
by the National Trust for Scotland,
lies just north of the village; a walk
through the wood leads to **Castle
Campbell**.

DOUNE
Central

On A84 8m NW of Stirling.

Once the centre of a thriving small-
arms industry, this picturesque
village is now quieter and more
peaceful. A bridge, said to have
been built by James IV's tailor
after a ferryman had refused him
passage, leads to **Doune Castle**.

DOUNE CASTLE
Doune, Central

Off A84 at Doune 8m NW of Stirling.
Apr–Sept, Mon–Sat 0930–1900, Sun
1400–1900; Oct–Mar, Mon–Thurs, Sat
0930–1600 (closed alternate Sats), Sun
1400–1600. HS (031 244 3101).

An imposing ruin built around
the turn of the 14th century by the
Regents Albany and Murdoch. The
Earls of Moray later took possession
of the castle, and the most famous of
them, the 'Bonnie Earl', lived there.
The current Earl of Moray's splendid
collection of vintage and more
recent cars is housed in **Doune Motor
Museum**.

DOUNE MOTOR MUSEUM
Doune, Central

On A84 at Doune 8m NW of Stirling.
Apr–Oct, daily 1000–1700. D (P)
(0786 841203).

Hispano-Suiza, Lagonda and Aston
Martin are among the famous
names to be found in Doune Motor
Museum, owned by the Earl of
Moray. The cars may be seen not
only on display, but also, during
Hill Climbs, being driven around:
the bulk of the collection is still in
working order.

DRUMCOLTRAN TOWER
near Dumfries, Dumfries and
Galloway

Off A711 8m SW of Dumfries. Apr–Sept,
Mon–Sat 0930–1900; Sun 1400–1900;
Oct–Mar, Mon–Sat 0930–1600, Sun
1400–1600. Free. Apply to key-keeper. HS
(031–244 3101).

A characteristically austere Scottish
tower-house, Drumcoltran dates
from the middle of the 16th century.

DRUMLANRIG CASTLE AND COUNTRY PARK
near Thornhill, Dumfries and
Galloway

Off A76, 3m N of Thornhill, Dumfriesshire.
Grounds: daily 28 Apr–30 Sept. Castle: 5
May–19 Aug, Mon–Sat 1100–1700, Sun
1400–1800. D (P) (0848 30248).

The imposing sandstone castle, built
in the late 17th century, houses an
impressive collection of paintings,
which includes works by Leonardo,
Rembrandt and Holbein. The
country park contains an adventure
play area and woodland walks.

DUMBARTON
Strathclyde

On A82 3m W of Erskine Bridge.

Once the capital of the ancient
kingdom of Strathclyde, Dumbarton
– the name is a corruption of *Dun
Breatann*, 'the fortress of the Britons'
– has the longest recorded history
as a fortified site of anywhere in
Britain. Dumbarton Rock, one of the
most recognizable landmarks on the
River **Clyde**, has been occupied since
the fifth century AD. The town has
of course expanded since those days,
and is no longer based around the
castle and the rock, which are about
a mile south-east of the current
town centre. The castle barracks are
mainly of modern construction –
they stayed in use into this century
– but much of greater age remains,
including mementos of Mary Queen
of Scots, who used Dumbarton as a
safe haven before fleeing to France.
In Castle Street in the town itself,
the Denny Ship Model Experiment
Tank is preserved as it was a
century ago, when scale wax and
wooden models of ships' hulls and
propellers would be tested; it is still
possible to see – and participate in –
the model-making process.

DUMFRIES
Dumfries and Galloway

Off A75.

The largest town in the Region,
Dumfries once occupied a central
place in Scottish politics, notably
in 1306, when Robert the Bruce
murdered John Comyn, his rival to

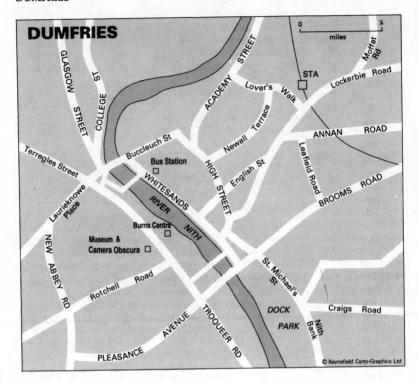

Town plan of Dumfries

the Scottish throne, in the church of the Minorite Friars. Bruce, excommunicated for the act, was proclaimed king at Scone two months later. But while its position astride the Border approaches gave Dumfries a degree of importance, inevitably, once peace with England had been agreed, the town's strategic significance declined. **Robert Burns** spent the last years of his life here with his wife Jean Armour; he moved to the town in 1790, taking up a post as exciseman, and died in 1796. He is buried in St Michael's churchyard along with his wife and five of their children; an early 19th-century mausoleum – bright blue, not in the most restrained taste – now stands over their graves. The Globe Inn off the High Street, the poet's favourite pub, contains some Burnsiana, including an inscribed window-pane. The Scottish Tourist Board's Burns heritage trail runs through the town; its major feature is the **Robert Burns Centre** in Mill Road. The best place to get an overview of life in Dumfries down the centuries is in Old Bridge House, at Devorgilla's Bridge: its rooms are furnished in the style of different eras. The bridge itself, dating from 1431, is one of the oldest surviving constructions in town. A mile south of the town centre off the B725, Crichton Royal Museum, in the hospital grounds, documents the history of the hospital and, by extension, of medicine in the UK. Exhibits include patients' art from the last century, and an operating theatre.

An out-of-the-way village today, Dunadd was once capital of the ancient Scots kingdom of Dalriada. Cairns, old churches, Celtic crosses and other artefacts can be found in abundance in Dunadd and the surrounding area, a testimony to the settlement's importance from the time it was first inhabited, estimated to be 4000 years ago, to the unification of Scotland under Kenneth MacAlpin in the ninth century AD.

DUNBLANE
Central

On A9 6m N of Stirling.

A small, affluent town on the Allan Water, Dunblane grew up around its cathedral. A place of worship has existed on the site of the cathedral since the start of the seventh century, when the Celtic Church of St Blane was founded. The tower of the current building dates from the 12th century, and was founded by David I; the rest was constructed a century later. The whole building fell into disrepair after the Reformation, but was restored from 1892 to 1895. There is a museum and library in the cathedral close. The well-known Dunblane Hydro hotel is in the town. At nearby Sheriffmuir, a battle in 1715 between the Jacobite Earl of Mar and the crown forces was fought, but Mar's subsequent retreat to Perth was instrumental in the failure of the uprising.

DUNADD
Strathclyde

Off A816 4m NW of Lochgilphead.

DUNDONALD CASTLE
near Kilmarnock, Strathclyde

Off A759 4½m SW of Kilmarnock.

Both King Robert II and his son Robert III died at isolated Dundonald, which may be viewed from the outside only. Although dilapidated, much of the castle's tower and outer wall still stands.

DUNDRENNAN ABBEY
near Kirkcudbright, Dumfries and Galloway

On A711 7m SE of Kirkcudbright. Apr–Sept, Mon–Sat 0930–1900, Sun 1400–1900; Oct–Mar, Mon–Sat 0930–1600, Sun 1400–1600. HS (031–244 3101).

A now-ruined Cistercian abbey, Dundrennan is said to be where Mary Queen of Scots spent her last night in her own country, in May 1568.

DUNOON
Strathclyde

On A815 SE Cowal peninsula.

Best reached by ferry from **Greenock**, across the **River Clyde**, Dunoon is the 'capital' of the Cowal peninsula, a sparsely populated part of the country speckled with picturesque villages. Dunoon has long been a traditional holiday resort for west-coast Scots, particularly in August, when it hosts the Cowal Highland Gathering. The nearby Holy Loch has long been home to a United States nuclear submarine base: while the existence of such an institution has provoked sporadic protest, its imminent closure appears likely to have a severely damaging effect on the local economy.

DUNSTAFFNAGE CASTLE AND CHAPEL
near Oban, Strathclyde

Off A85 4m N of Oban. Apr–Sept, Mon–Sat 0930–1900, Sun 1400–1900; Oct–Mar, Mon–Wed, Sat 0930–1600, Thurs 0930–1300, Sun 1400–1600. HS (031–244 3101).

The 13th-century castle is still in good condition. The chapel nearby is ruined, but what remains is a tantalizing reminder of the original grandeur.

DUNURE CASTLE
near Ayr, Strathclyde

On A719 6m SW of Ayr. All year. Daily.

An attractive ruin, Dunure is infamous as the site of the roasting alive of the Commendator of **Crossraguel Abbey**. The perpetrators were the powerful Cassillis family, engaged in an attempt to seize the abbey lands. There is a picnic area just by the castle.

DURISDEER
Dumfries and Galloway

Off A702 5m NE of Drumlanrig.

The village's 17th-century church contains the Queensberry Aisle, a picturesque mausoleum which in turn contains a memorial to the 2nd Duke and Duchess of Queensberry.

EASTWOOD BUTTERFLY KINGDOM
Giffnock, Strathclyde

Rouken Glen Park, Rouken Glen Road, Giffnock, off A77 at Eastwood Toll. Late Mar–early Nov, daily 1000–1700. D (041–620 2084).

A tropical garden houses a colourful collection of free-flying butterflies and moths, while the insectarium – behind glass – contains scorpions, spiders, and giant millipedes. More comfortingly familiar creatures, such as rabbits, budgerigars and hamsters, may be found in the pet centre.

ECCLEFECHAN
Dumfries and Galloway

Off A74 5½m SE of Lockerbie.

The village of Ecclefechan is best known as the birthplace of the historian and man of letters Thomas Carlyle (1795–1881). Carlyle's birthplace, now owned by the National Trust for Scotland, is an arched house built by his father and uncle a few years before he was born; it contains an extensive collection of his manuscripts and belongings.

EGLINTON COUNTRY PARK
near Irvine, Strathclyde

Off A78 2m N of Irvine. All year. Daily. Visitor centre: 1000–1630; country park: 0900–1700. Free (0294 51776).

The extensive, landscaped park includes nature trails and picnic sites; the visitor centre includes

displays on the natural history of the area, and on the most famous event to take place on the site, the mock-medieval Eglinton Tournament of 1839.

ELECTRIC BRAE
near Ayr, Strathclyde

On A719 9m S of Ayr.

A famous, befuddling road, Electric Brae is the site of an optical illusion which makes travellers think they are going down the hill when in fact they are going up. The trip here used to be a popular family excursion.

ELLISLAND FARM
near Dumfries, Dumfries and Galloway

Off A76 6m NW of Dumfries. All year, phone to arrange. D (P). Free (0387 74 426).

Home to **Robert Burns** from 1788 to 1791, a period during which he wrote some of his best works, among them 'Tam O' Shanter', Ellisland houses a display in the granary. The farmhouse, built by Burns himself, contains a museum.

FALKIRK
Central

Off M9 10m SE of Stirling.

As it is the midpoint of the Edinburgh-**Glasgow** rail link, Falkirk has evolved into a sizeable dormitory town for both cities, the journey either way taking 25 minutes. Nearby **Grangemouth** with its docks and oil refinery is the main local source of work. The **Antonine Wall** passed nearby the town, and Falkirk Museum, in Orchard Street, contains displays relating to the erstwhile Roman frontier. Two significant battles were staged in the town: in 1298, a Scottish army under William Wallace lost a battle here to King Edward I of England during the early stages of the **Wars of Independence**, while, in 1746, the retreating forces of Bonnie Prince Charlie had one of their last successes against the government troops.

FOOTBALL, see panel p99.

FORTH AND CLYDE CANAL,
see panel p100.

FURNACE
Strathclyde

On A83 8m SW of Inveraray.

On the shores of Loch Fyne, almost equidistant from **Auchindrain** and **Crarae Garden**, Furnace takes its name from the smelting furnace which, in the 18th century, used trees from the area which had been felled to give less cover to fugitive Jacobites.

Football: The National Weakness

While rugby holds sway in the Borders, and shinty predominates in the Highlands and northern Strathclyde, football alone can really claim to be the Scottish national game. Scotland's per capita attendance at football matches is the second highest in Europe, behind Albania, and the sport – with 38 'senior' clubs organized into three divisions – is followed so fervently by some that it can often seem to be the most important activity in their lives. The increasing popularity of fanzines – amateur publications produced by supporters, usually for little or no profit – attests to the fact that the commitment of a significant proportion of fans extends way beyond 90 minutes on a Saturday afternoon.

Football was first organized into league and cup competitions in Britain, and the **Glasgow** side Queen's Park could hold their own against the best teams from south of the Border. Understandably, once the sport spread throughout the world, countries with greater populations – and hence more players to choose from – overtook the Scots in terms of ability. All the same, most supporters still expect the national side to play with the uninhibited, natural talent which they regard as their birthright.

Whole advertising campaigns – particularly on health matters – have tried to latch on to the Scottish obsession with football: one in the late 1970s stated 'Visit your dentist regularly – and that means more regularly than Scotland win the World Cup.' The serious side of the sport is that it remains a focus for Protestant–Catholic sectarianism, particularly in Glasgow, where the Rangers–Celtic rivalry is well known. Matters have recently improved in this respect, however, and in 1989 Rangers' signing of Maurice Johnston – their first big-name Roman Catholic player, who has since moved on to Everton in England – has helped to diminish the importance of religion in the sport.

The Forth and Clyde Canal

The Forth and Clyde Canal stretches from **Grangemouth**, on the River Forth, to Bowling, on the River **Clyde**, as well as having a two-mile branch into **Glasgow**. Thirty-five miles long, it was begun at Grangemouth in 1768, and was completed at its western end in 1790. The canal served a triple purpose: it allowed sea-going vessels to go from one side of Scotland to the other without having to go round the top of the country, which was far more time-consuming and often perilous; it was used to transport goods from one part of central Scotland to another; and it also served as passenger transport, connecting with coach services. Steamboats and puffers were a common sight on the canal throughout the 19th and into the 20th centuries, and even a midget submarine turned up in 1952. En route from the Clyde to the Forth, this rare visitor caused some consternation, not to mention wild rumours, among the people living by the banks of the canal.

With goods and passengers long since having taken to the roads or the rail network, the canal was closed in 1963, and there followed a decade in which it fell into disrepair. Many sections were simply neglected, while others were filled in and had new roads built over them. But as the condition of the canal deteriorated, so a campaign to restore it grew: increased activity throughout the 1970s saw pressure groups take to the water in canoes and other small craft. Largely due to voluntary workers, the canal has been cleaned up, and half the length of its towpath resurfaced. Although still a relatively underused facility, the canal today offers many leisure activities, from fishing to marathon canoe races, as well as being home to many species of wildlife, such as mallards, mink, frogs, toads, and the majestic grey heron.

GALLOWAY FOREST PARK
Dumfries and Galloway

Off A714 10m NW of Newton Stewart. All year. D (P). Free (0671 2420).

The Forestry Commission owns this 250-square-mile site, which contains the Merrick, at 2765 feet the highest hill, as opposed to mountain, in southern Scotland. Galloway Deer Museum, by Clatteringshaws Loch, provides information about deer, other wildlife, and the natural history of the region. There are forest walks of varying degrees of difficulty throughout the park, as well as Raiders Road, a 10-mile drive.

GARTMORN DAM
near Alloa, Central

Off A908, by Sauchie, 2m NE of Alloa. Park: all year, daily. Visitor centre: Apr–Sept, daily 0830–1730; Oct–Mar, Sat–Sun 1400–1600. D (P). Free (0259 214319).

This country park and nature reserve includes the oldest dam in Scotland. Fishing is permissible in the reservoir, and the visitor centre provides more information about the area.

GATEHOUSE OF FLEET
Dumfries and Galloway

Off A75 8m NW of Kirkcudbright.

A pleasant, tranquil town today, Gatehouse of Fleet was an important cotton-mill centre from the mid 18th–mid 19th centuries. The local laird, James Murray, who commissioned his Italianate residence, Cally House, planned the building of the new town and its mills. The **Mill on the Fleet** visitor centre records his achievement. Now dependent on agriculture and tourism, the town has been designated an area of outstanding natural beauty, and, like nearby **Kirkcudbright**, is popular with visiting artists. **Venniehill** has a viewpoint which can be reached from the town.

GIGHA, ISLE OF
Strathclyde

Off Kintyre.

Lying just west of the Kintyre peninsula, this small, flat island (pronounced Ghee-ya) is accessible by ferry from **Tayinloan**. Warmed by the Gulf Stream, its waters are a renowned source of shellfish. The ruined church at Kilchattan dates from the 13th century.

GIGHA, ACHAMORE HOUSE GARDENS

All year. Daily, 1000–dusk. D (P).

The mild climate on the island of Gigha was indispensable to the development of Achamore House Gardens, which contain camellias, rhododendrons and some semi-tropical species; Achamore House itself is not open to the public.

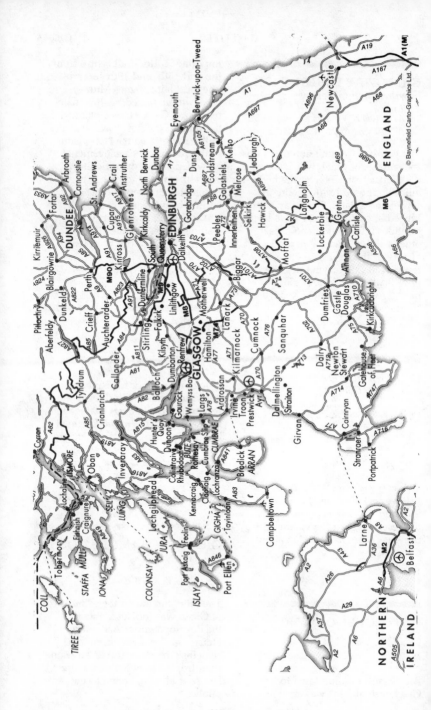

GILNOCKIE TOWER
near Langholm, Dumfries and Galloway

Off A7 5m S of Langholm. All year. Free (03873 80976).

This 16th-century tower, which can be viewed from the outside only, was one of the homes of Johnnie Armstrong, the most famous – or infamous – of the Border reivers or raiders.

GIRVAN
Strathclyde

On B719 8m S of Turnberry.

A busy seaside town in season, Girvan was once a fishing port, but now relies chiefly on tourism. Its sandy beach and sporting facilities – indoor swimming, bowls and tennis, as well as the many golf courses in the area – still managing to attract families from the Glasgow area.

GLASGOW
Strathclyde

On M8 43 m W of Edinburgh.

The biggest city in Scotland by far (the second largest, Edinburgh, has roughly half the population), Glasgow dominates Scottish life in many respects, depite not being the capital. Much of the country's heavy industry has been centred on Glasgow, particularly on the **River Clyde**; and the bulk of the Scottish media is based there, including BBC Scotland. Like Edinburgh, Glasgow enjoys a number of arts festivals. The city held the title of European Capital of Culture in 1990. The annual Mayfest nurtures close links with community arts; Scottish Opera has been based in the city for more than 30 years; and – because of the concentration of population – there are more theatres, cinemas and music venues in Glasgow than anywhere else.

Although little of antiquity survives, the history of the city goes back to the middle of the sixth century, when St Mungo (also known as Kentigern) founded a monastery where **Glasgow Cathedral** now stands. The cathedral stood just up the hill from the heart of the old town, Glasgow Cross (even today it is less than a mile from the current city centre, George Square), and was the original base for **Glasgow University**. Glasgow played only a marginal role in the **Wars of Independence**, although it was near the city, in 1305, that Sir William Wallace was taken prisoner before being sent to England and hanged. The fall from power of Mary Queen of Scots was settled at the battle of Langside (now part of the city, on the South Side) in 1568.

The real rise to prominence, and to its position as the second city of the British empire, began for Glasgow in the early 18th century with the expansion of shipbuilding on the Clyde, and the huge growth of the tobacco industry, reflected today in such names as Virginia Street in the **Merchant City**, which was itself named after the tobacco lords and associated entrepreneurs. The shipbuilding industry expanded throughout the 18th and 19th centuries, until just before World War I Clydeside as a whole (in other words, including such ports as **Greenock** and **Clydebank**) was producing almost a third of the

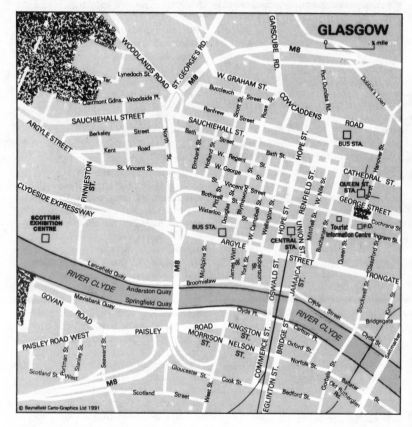

Town plan of Glasgow

world's entire output of steamships. Industrial expansion brought with it a substantial influx of newcomers, particularly from the Highlands, where many of the people had been cleared off the land to make way for the landowners' sheep, and Ireland, where the periodic failure of the potato crop meant there was a real risk of starvation.

No city in history has ever been free of poverty, but, by the inter-war era, Glasgow seemed to have more than its fair share. Its reputation as a warren of slums inhabited by rickets-ridden, razor-wielding ruffians began to grow around this time, and continued to do so after the war, when the mass construction of tower blocks to replace the old tenements only served to break up the old communities without improving the living standards of their members. Ironically, while the wealth generated throughout the world in the 1950s and 1960s seemed unable to improve Glasgow, it was only in the early 1980s, with unemployment at record heights and the old heavy industries in terminal decline – in other words, at a time when one might have expected Glasgow to appear even poorer and more depressed than before – that the regeneration of the city began. The 'Glasgow's Miles Better' slogan typified the first phase of the campaign to improve the morale of the citizens and the image of Glasgow held by outsiders. Funds were poured into new ventures such as the Merchant City, and millions of pounds were spent on the arts. By the late 1980s, when Glasgow was selected as the European Capital of Culture for 1990, public perception of the city had gone full circle: from being stereotyped as depressed and violent, it was now seen as friendly and full of vitality.

Any public image, of course, can never wholly coincide with the reality. Whole slabs of the city and its satellite towns still suffer from high unemployment and chronically substandard housing. All the same, Glasgow today has a new-found self-confidence. It is large enough to embrace some striking contrasts: the canyons of the city centre, especially at night, are reminiscent of the great American metropolises. Yet Glasgow also has the highest percentage of parkland of any European city. Regarded as a whole it does not have the same aesthetic appeal as Edinburgh; but the city boundaries do enclose many fine individual buildings, particularly from Victorian times. Glasgow's chief asset, however, is its people: stereotypes are sometimes based on fact, and certainly Glaswegians are as warm, and as willing to engage strangers in conversation, as the cliché would suggest.

GLASGOW, ART GALLERY AND MUSEUM

Kelvingrove Park. All year. Mon–Wed, Fri–Sat 1000–1700, Thurs 1000–2100, Sun 1200–1800. D. Free (041-357 3929).

Finished in 1901, this warm, welcoming, red sandstone structure is one of the best-loved buildings in the city, and houses a fine collection of Renaissance, Impressionist, Post-Impressionist and contemporary paintings. Local legend has it that Kelvingrove, as it is known, was built back to front, but it is more likely that the architects simply wanted the rear entrance, from Kelvingrove

The Glasgow Boys: Then And Now

The original group of artists to be called the Glasgow Boys
flourished in the last quarter of the 19th century. The
group, including Sir James Guthrie, Edward A. Hornel, Arthur
Melville, and Sir John Lavery, was not composed solely of
Glaswegians, but was named because, at one time or another,
all of its members worked in shared studios in the area of
Glasgow around Sauchiehall Street and St Vincent Street. At
first the group came in for much the same treatment from the
critics as was meted out shortly afterwards to **Charles Rennie
Mackintosh** – at best wilful miscomprehension of their work, at
worst outright hostility. Guthrie turned from genre to portraiture,
which was where Lavery, who was born in Belfast, also achieved
his greatest popular success.

The past decade has seen the rise of a new school of Glasgow
Boys, although these modern painters – Stephen Campbell,
Peter Howson, and Ken Currie being foremost among them –
perhaps do not have as much in common as the first group
did. Currie, for instance, at least in the first half of the 1980s,
produced work heavily influenced by the more socially committed
branch of German expressionism – nightmarishly vivid scenes of
working-class life – while Campbell's work is an obscure mélange
of mythologies, an amalgam of classical allusions and references
to the painter's own life. **Glasgow's Art Gallery and Museum**
contains examples of the new Glasgow Boys' work, although,
as they were acclaimed as something new and exciting almost
as soon as they graduated from art school, many of their best
paintings are already in the United States in private collections.
There is also a group of female artists which has been designated
the Glasgow Girls, affirming that the city has been one of the most
artistically productive in Britain.

Park (among the most popular of **Glasgow's green spaces**), to be as grand as the front. Salvador Dali's *Christ of St John of the Cross* is the best known of the exhibits: a controversial purchase in the 1960s, it is said to have since paid for itself and more by the number of postcard reproductions of it sold. The paintings range from Rubens and Rembrandt to works by the **Glasgow Boys** old and new; similarly, the sculptures on display include works by Rodin and Epstein, and by modern Scots such as Benno Schotz. Kelvingrove's museum section includes natural history displays, suits of armour and weaponry, and the geology of Scotland. There are also temporary exhibitions of both art and other themes.

GLASGOW, BOTANIC GARDEN AND KIBBLE PALACE

Off A82 on junction of Great Western Road and Byres Road. All year: Gardens: 0700–dusk. Kibble Palace 1000–1645, Main Range: Mon–Sat 1300–1645, Sun 1200–1645. Oct–Mar closes 1615 daily. D. Free (041–334 2422).

One of the most popular of **Glasgow's green spaces**, the Botanic Garden includes a chronological border, which shows in which century plants were introduced to Britain, a herb garden, and, in the glasshouses, a renowned collection of orchids. The Kibble Palace is the oldest of the gardens' glasshouses, and houses tree ferns and other temperate plants. The gardens are often used, in summer, as a venue for television programmes by the BBC, whose Scottish headquarters are just across the road in Queen Margaret Drive.

GLASGOW BOYS, see panel p106.

GLASGOW, BURRELL COLLECTION

Pollok Country Park, off Pollokshaws Road. All year. Mon–Tues, Thurs–Sat, 1000–1700, Wed 1000–2200, Sun 1200–1800. D. Free (041–649 7151).

Opened in 1983, the collection has quickly established itself as one of the most popular venues for visitors in Scotland, although the building itself, an eclectic glass and brick construction, has not met with unanimous acclaim. The collection was bequeathed to the city by Sir William Burrell (1861–1958), a shipping tycoon and inveterate collector of ceramics, stained glass, pictures, furniture, and more; Burrell himself seems to have given pride of place to his medieval French tapestries, and to his collection of Oriental objects: bronzes, ceramics, and works in terracotta. The collection of paintings, drawings and prints – frequently augmented by temporary exhibitions – is particularly strong on 19th-century French artists, but also includes works by Bellini and Rembrandt. The Burrell stands roughly in the middle of Pollok Country Park, a sprawling area which includes playing fields, grazing land for Highland cattle, and **Pollok House**.

GLASGOW, CITY CHAMBERS

George Square. All year. Mon–Fri, tours at 1030 and 1430 or by arrangement. D. Free (041–227 4017/8).

Those visitors who still subscribe to the notion of Glasgow as a nightmarish amalgam of tower blocks and motorways would be well advised to start off their stay in the city with a tour of the City Chambers, the headquarters of Glasgow District Council. The competition-winning design by William Young, in Italian Renaissance style, was opened by Queen Victoria in 1888 – a year before another great Italianate building, **Templeton's Carpet Factory**. The opulence of the interior – wide, marble staircases, sumptuous chandeliers – gives the impression of indomitable civic confidence, which, indeed, was the intention: the building was designed as an attempt to restore the self-belief of the city fathers after the disastrous crash of the City of Glasgow Bank.

GLASGOW, CROOKSTON CASTLE

Brockburn Road, off Crookston Road, 4m SW of city centre. All year. Opening by arrangement with the key-keeper. HS (031–244 3101).

Built on the site of a 12th-century castle, Crookston is a tower-house constructed in the early 15th century. Mary Queen of Scots, and the ill-fated Lord Darnley stayed here after their marriage in 1565.

GLASGOW, FOSSIL GROVE

Victoria Park Drive North, facing Airthrey Avenue. Open by arrangement. D. Free (041–959 2128).

In Victoria Park, Fossil Grove contains the fossil stumps and roots

of trees estimated to be 330 million years old.

GLASGOW, GLASGOW CATHEDRAL

At E end of Cathedral Street. Apr–Sept, Mon–Sat 0930–1900, Sun 1400–1900; Oct–Mar, Mon–Sat 0930–1600, Sun 1400–1600. D (P). Free. HS (031–244 3101).

Only a few hundred yards up the High Street from what was the centre of the old town at Glasgow Cross, the astmospheric cathedral houses the tomb of St Mungo, Glasgow's patron saint, who died in 603. Fragments remain from the 12th century, but the bulk of the surviving building dates from the 13th century. This is the most complete example of Gothic churches in the south of Scotland.

GLASGOW, GLASGOW SCHOOL OF ART

167 Renfrew Street. Daily in term-time or by arrangement. D (P). Free (041–332 9797).

Designed by **Charles Rennie Mackintosh** in 1896, and completed in 1909, the art school is widely regarded as his masterpiece. It was built in two phases, as is shown by the different styles of the east and west elevations, the former resembling a tower-house, the latter a unique flurry of glass bays. The school's museum contains a collection of Mackintosh material, while the library is one of his most effective achievements in the Celtic twilight style.

Glasgow's Green Spaces

For a city with a long tradition of heavy industry, Glasgow is blessed with a very large number of green spaces; it is, in fact, said to have the highest percentage of parkland of any European city. This has, of course, come under threat, especially from proposals to construct new roads or build extensions to existing ones. The oldest public park in the city, Glasgow Green, has been under most threat in recent years, but for the moment is safe. Along with the **People's Palace** museum which stands on it, Glasgow Green is a powerful symbol of the working-class city. It was originally the common pasture for the embryonic town: even now, one of the privileges granted when someone is made a freeman of the city is the right to graze cattle on the Green. In more recent times it was the scene of fights between rival gangs, or just between individuals settling their differences. In the South Side of the city, Pollok Country Park is a 365-acre site which includes both the **Burrell Collection** and **Pollok House**, as well as a herd of Highland cattle, a demonstration garden, and sundry playing fields. Also in the South Side is Bellahouston Park, scene of the 1937 Empire Exhibition and one of the places visited by the Pope in 1982. One of the most popular of the city's green spaces is the **Botanic Garden** in **Glasgow's West End**, a part of town which also takes in Kelvingrove Park, a partially wooded expanse on each side of the River Kelvin, and a popular spot to walk in before or after a visit to the nearby **Art Gallery and Museum**.

GLASGOW, GLASGOW UNIVERSITY

*University Avenue, 2m NW of city
centre. Visitor centre: May–Oct, Mon–Sat
0930–1700, Sun 1400–1700; Nov–Apr,
Mon–Fri 0930–1700, Sat 0930–1300. D (P).
Free (041-330 5511).*

Founded in 1451, the university was
originally attached to the Blackfriars
Kirk and then to Glasgow cathedral,
before moving into buildings off
the High Street. The move to its
current site at Gilmorehill was
made possible by the acquisition
of land there in 1865; work on
the new building, designed by Sir
George Gilbert Scott, was begun
the following year. The visitor
centre has exhibitions of university
life, and video displays. Tours are
organized from the visitor centre.

GLASGOW, GLASGOW ZOOPARK
Calderpark, Uddingston

*Off A74 6m SE of city centre. All year.
Daily, summer 1000–1800, winter
1000–1700. D (P) (041-771 2615).*

Outdoors, lions, monkeys, black
bears, white rhinos and the only
white tiger in Scotland roam around
in their enclosures and paddocks;
indoors, the tropical reptile house
is home to snakes and lizards, as
well as tortoises. Many of the rare
animals are involved in a captive
breeding programme; Père David's
deer, for instance, were reintroduced
into the wild in 1986 due partly to
work done in Calderpark, which
continues to house and breed the
species.

GLASGOW'S GREEN SPACES,
see panel p109.

GLASGOW, HAGGS CASTLE

*100 St Andrew's Drive. All year. Mon–Sat
1000–1700, Sun 1200–1800. D. Free
(041-427 2725).*

Built in 1585 by the Maxwells,
Haggs Castle stayed in that family
until it was abandoned in 1732
and became a ruin. Restored last
century, it was opened as a public
museum, designed especially for
children, in 1976. School groups
visit daily in term-time, and a great
variety of workshops is available
during the holidays. Some of the
rooms have been reconverted to
show what life was like in centuries
past, and the garden attempts to
replicate the state of Scottish castle
gardens at the time that Haggs
was built.

GLASGOW, HUNTERIAN ART GALLERY

*82 Hillhead Street. All year. Mon–Fri
0930–1700, Sat 1400–1700. D (P). Free
(041-330 5431).*

The Hunterian's fine collection of
Scottish art includes the leading
Colourists, with works on show by
Samuel John Peploe, Joan Eardley,
William McTaggart and John
Duncan Fergusson. The international
collection includes paintings by
Rembrandt and Camille Pissarro,
along with a fine selection of works
by James Whistler, unmatched
outside Washington. The gallery
also includes the Mackintosh House,

Glasgow's Merchant City

In one episode of *No Mean City*, the 1930s pulp classic of Glasgow fiction by Alexander McArthur and H. Kingsley Long, the anti-hero 'Razor King', having slashed three rivals in the centre of town, makes good his escape from the police. Turning into Glassford Street, he runs past an area of warehouses and coal depots; by the time he reaches Candleriggs he has outpaced his pursuers and, by now just walking, crosses the **River Clyde** to his Gorbals home. Were Mr King to flee by the same route today, the scenery he passed would be changed beyond recognition. In that part of town whose boundaries are George Street, High Street, Argyle Street and Queen Street, the changes have been more dramatic, perhaps, than in any other urban renewal project in Britain. Only a decade ago, there was no Merchant City. Now, its restored warehouses and new developments are home to around 2000 people; its 70 acres contain some of the city's most popular pubs and eating places; and it is the most potent symbol of the 'new Glasgow' – celebrated by the Labour-controlled district council, who initiated its renewal by attracting private funds, and vilified by the city's vociferous hard left.

Although it takes its name from the fact that many of the 18th-century tobacco merchants based themselves in its southern streets, conveniently close to the Clyde, the Merchant City is, in essence, a creation of Glasgow District Council's public relations department. The impetus for the venture, which has so far seen approximately £12 million of public money spent on it, began around the start of the 1980s. About a third of the property in the area was then vacant or unused; and a similar proportion of all property – including two-thirds of the vacant property – was owned by the district council. At the same time as Lord Provost Michael Kelly was beginning his successful 'Glasgow's Miles Better' publicity drive, private firms began accepting conversion grants from the council averaging £5100 for every house created. The Albion Buildings at 60 Ingram Street, planning permission for which was granted in June 1982, became the first new housing in the Merchant City area for over a century. Old warehouses became new flats; smaller, often derelict buildings were transformed into bars, inns or restaurants; and people began to move back to the centre of Glasgow.

a lovingly detailed reconstruction of **Charles Rennie Mackintosh**'s nearby residence in Florentine Terrace.

GLASGOW, HUNTERIAN MUSEUM

University Avenue. All year. Mon–Fri 0930–1700, Sat 0930–1300 (May–Oct, Sat until 1700), Sun 1400–1700. D (P). Free (041-330 4221).

Opened in 1807, the Hunterian is the oldest public museum in Scotland. William Hunter (1718–83), whose endowment of £8000 established the museum, was a pioneering anatomist and obstetrician – so pioneering, indeed, that he is believed to have been party to body-snatching in an attempt always to have corpses to hand for his experiments. (A replica in the museum of a 1773 engraving shows him being caught in the act of stealing a woman's body.) The museum includes a coin gallery, and substantial sections on geology, archaeology, and ethnography, along with a display on the Romans in Scotland, which includes artefacts from the **Antonine Wall**. The display on the history of the university includes many fascinating, if gruesome, stories from the early days of medical science.

GLASGOW, HUTCHESONS' HALL

158 Ingram Street, near SE corner of George Square. All year. Mon–Fri 0900–1700, Sat 1000–1600. D (P). Free. NTS (041-552 8391).

The regional offices of the National Trust for Scotland, Hutchesons' Hall

was built from 1802 to 1805. Named after the brothers George and Thomas, who founded Hutchesons' Hospital in the 17th century, the Hall includes statues of them on its frontage. There is a visitor centre and a Trust shop, and function rooms available for private hire.

GLASGOW'S MERCHANT CITY, see panel p111.

GLASGOW, MITCHELL LIBRARY

North Street. All year. Mon–Fri 1930–2100, Sat 0930–1700. D. Free (041-221 7030).

The biggest public reference library in Europe, the Mitchell contains over a million volumes. The grand original building (1906–11), with its distinctive dome and sweeping marble staircase, was incorporated into an enlargement in the 1970s. Each part is aesthetically acceptable in its own terms, yet, almost inevitably, the two together are a less than perfect marriage. The Glasgow Room is the place to go for anyone wishing to explore the city's history. The Mitchell also includes what is believed to be the largest collection in the world of books and documents on **Robert Burns**.

GLASGOW, MUSEUM OF TRANSPORT

Kelvin Hall, 1 Bunhouse Road, off Argyle Street. All year. Mon–Fri 1000–1700, Sat 1000–2200, Sun 1200–1800. D. Free (041-357 3929).

Modern Glasgow in Print

Even now, the book that would receive most nominations as the quintessential **Glasgow** novel is *No Mean City* by Alexander McArthur and H. Kingsley Long. A moralistic tale of the rise and fall of a Gorbals gang-leader, it has sold well ever since its original publication in 1935. Although frowned on by many Glaswegians because of its stereotypical depiction of the city's poor as, in the main, violent, amoral drunkards, it is a fast-moving tale, and the modern reader who knows the city will be fascinated to find out about its geography and social conditions six decades ago. Today, more accomplished Glaswegian writers dominate Scottish literature. The novels and stories of James Kelman are uncompromising accounts of ordinary life, sometimes grim, but frequently possessed of an understated humour. Alasdair Gray, by contrast, mixes realism with episodes of fantasy, most notably in his best-known work, the novel *Lanark* (the title refers to the central character, not to the town). William McIlvanney sets novels such as *Docherty* in his home town of **Kilmarnock** under the name of Graithnock; his novels about the policeman Laidlaw, however, are set in the city. Occasionally vilified as a romanticizer of old-fashioned machismo, McIlvanney produces serious, thoughtful fiction in a popular form. Three poets, at least, are worth mentioning. Liz Lochhead specializes in acerbic observations of the douce middle class; the veteran Edwin Morgan writes many short poems, often about specific locations within the city; while Tom Leonard, less well known than the other two, is the author of a small body of work, some concrete poetry, some monologues in dialect, best appreciated in live performance.

Bicycles, motorbikes, cars, ships, buses and trams are all packed into the museum, a nostalgic delight for adults, and an exciting venue for children. The reconstruction of an old Glasgow street is among the most evocative exhibits: the shop fronts are all stocked with period wares, and there is even a small cinema which you can walk into.

GLASGOW, NECROPOLIS

Behind Glasgow Cathedral. Daily, summer 0900–2100, winter 0900–1700. D (P). Free (041–771 6372).

Begun in 1833 and modelled on the famous Père Lachaise cemetery in Paris, the Necropolis is as close to being a celebration of material wealth as it is possible for a burial ground to be. So many wealthy Glaswegians of the last century, deciding to go out with a bang and be buried in a splendid tomb, chose this site; the most notable example is the Menteith Mausoleum of 1842. Even the stern statue of John Knox, overlooking not only the Necropolis but much of the eastern side of the city, fails to make the place seem as so sombre as cemeteries usually are.

GLASGOW, PEOPLE'S PALACE

In Glasgow Green. All year. Mon–Sat 1000–1700. Sun 1200–1800. D (P). Free (041–554 0223).

From a miner's pit boots to Billy Connolly's big banana boots, from a reconstruction of a tobacconist's shop to banners depicting the history of the trade union movement, the museum celebrates the social history and heritage of the city and its people in a collection which is both humorous and moving.

GLASGOW, POLLOK HOUSE

Pollok Country Park, off Pollokshaws Road. All year. Mon–Tues, Thurs–Sat 1000–1700, Wed 1000–2200, Sun 1200–1800. D (P). Free (041–632 0274).

Built around the middle of the 18th century as a private residence for the Maxwell family, Pollok House (and the country park, among the most notable of **Glasgow's green spaces**) was given to the city in 1966. It now houses the Stirling Maxwell collection of Spanish and other European paintings, as well as works by British artists, among them William Blake. There are displays of furniture and decorations from the time of the house's construction. Within the original walled garden, a demonstration garden has been designed for amateur horticulturists. The **Burrell Collection** is also in the country park.

GLASGOW, PROVAND'S LORDSHIP

Castle Street, opposite the cathedral. All year. Mon–Sat 1000–1900, Sun 1200–1800. D (P). Free (041–552 8819).

Apart from the cathedral, this is the only remaining medieval building in the city. Built in 1471 as a manse, it is now a museum, chiefly devoted to artefacts from the Middle Ages – furniture, armoury, religious relics – in addition to a number of exhibits pertaining to Glasgow's street characters of the last century.

GLASGOW, PROVAN HALL

Auchinlea Road, Easterhouse, off M8, 3m E of city centre. D. Free. NTS (041–552 839)1

Provan Hall itself may currently be seen from the outside only. Built in the 15th century, it is an outstanding example of the pre-Reformation mansion house, typically Scottish in its austerity.

GLASGOW, ROYAL INTERNATIONAL CONCERT HALL

Buchanan Street (041–332 3123).

Constructed for the city's reign as European Capital of Culture, the building has been subjected to some criticism by those who regard its architecture as inappropriate for a Scottish city centre. Controversy also arose over a prize-winning mural donated by Strathclyde Region: deemed unsuitable by Glasgow District Council, the offending artwork was covered by curtains before eventually being removed. The acoustics, however, have met with an almost universally favourable response, and the concert hall is already established as a leading venue for all types of classical and popular music.

GLASGOW, SCOTLAND STREET SCHOOL

225 Scotland Street. All year. Mon–Sat 1000–1700, Sun 1400–1700. Free (041–429 1202).

Designed by **Charles Rennie Mackintosh** in 1904, Scotland Street School is such an attractive building that even the most recalcitrant elementary school pupil may just have enjoyed attending. From the outside its turrets give it the appearance of a toytown fort, while the interior – in particular the drill hall – is one of the best examples of Mackintosh's mastery of light and space. The school is now an education museum, in which classrooms have been reconstructed in the style of certain periods, all as they would have been on 20 June of a given year. The classroom for 1891 contains a dunce's cap, sitting patiently in the corner awaiting a wearer; in 1940, the pupils are about to receive instructions for evacuation. There are films of children's games of the past, and today's young visitors can borrow old toys to play with in the building or out in the playground.

GLASGOW, SPRINGBURN MUSEUM AND EXHIBITION CENTRE

Ayr Street, off A803. All year. Mon–Fri 1030–1700, Sat 1000–1630, Sun 1400–1700. D. Free (041–557 1405).

This award-winning social history museum records the life of the local community, which centred on the railway works. By the late 1890s Springburn was the largest centre in the world for the manufacture of steam locomotives.

GLASGOW, TEMPLETON'S CARPET FACTORY

Off Glasgow Green.

Still known by its old name although it is now a business

centre, the erstwhile carpet factory was built in 1889, and is a copy of the Doge's Palace in Venice – an extraordinary sight to come across on the fringes of the city's East End, where most of the architecture is council housing. Although Templeton's has been denigrated by some as preposterous pastiche, Glaswegians generally regard it with great affection. The building may currently be viewed from the outside only.

GLASGOW, THE TENEMENT HOUSE

145 Buccleuch Street, Garnethill, N of Charing Cross. 1 Apr–28 Oct, daily 1200–1700; 3 Nov–1 Apr, Sat–Sun 1400–1600. NTS (041-333 0183).

The flat, on the first floor of the building, exemplifies life in one of the city's superior residential districts in the early decades of this century. The tenement was built in 1892, and the Towards, mother and daughter, moved in in 1911, living there for over 50 years. Their name is still on the door, and many of the artefacts inside belonged to them. The ground floor flat has displays about the house, and doubles as a ticket office.

GLASGOW'S WEST END, see panel p117.

GLENLUCE ABBEY
near Glenluce, Dumfries and Galloway

Off A75 2m N of Glenluce. Apr–Sept, Mon–Sat 0930–1900, Sun 1400–1900;

Oct–Mar, Mon–Sat 0930–1600, Sun 1400–1600. D (P) HS (031-244 3101).

Founded towards the close of the 12th century, this now-ruined abbey was once home to Cistercian monks.

GOUROCK
Strathclyde

On A770 25m NW of Glasgow.

Now in effect a western continuation of **Greenock**. Gourock stands on a head of land where the **River Clyde** turns sharply south. The town naturally has a strong seafaring tradition, and the Kempock Stone, in the Castle Mansions overlooking the Clyde, is named after Granny Kempock, by legend a beneficent witch who had power over the sea. Fishermen about to sail forth into the firth would ask for her blessing, as would newly married couples. Neither Granny nor that tradition, however, was as old as the stone itself, which is believed to have performed a similar function since prehistoric times. Ferries travel from Gourock to **Dunoon** on the Cowal peninsula.

GRANGEMOUTH
Central

Off M9 5m E of Falkirk.

A gloomy-looking industrial town by day, Grangemouth is seen at its best from the mainline train between Glasgow and Edinburgh at night, when the steel constructions, lit by the flames from the oil refinery, look awesomely modern, a spaceage megalopolis. The docks and refinery are a major source of employment for the **Falkirk** area.

Glasgow's West End

An inexact area, the West End may be said to stretch from Woodlands Road just off Charing Cross to Hyndland and Kelvinside, taking in Hillhead, Kelvinbridge, and Dowanhill. Its centre is Byres Road, primarily a shopping street with a few good pubs along it, but the real reason for the continued vitality of the West End is **Glasgow University**: thousands of its students choose to live in the area. The quality of housing differs widely from street to street; turn a corner and the price of the properties has doubled; the result is that the West End community is a melting pot of the well-off and the less affluent. Many of the most interesting venues in Glasgow are within the West End: the **Art Gallery and Museum** at Kelvingrove; the **Museum of Transport** just across the road; and the **Hunterian Museum** and **Hunterian Gallery**, both attached to the university. Two of the best-known of **Glasgow's green spaces** are also in the West End: the **Botanic Garden** and Kelvingrove Park.

Every section of the city has its partisans, consisting mainly of those who grew up in the area and see no reason to live elsewhere; South-Siders, for example, are fiercely loyal to their largely residential part of the town, while for many of those who live north of the river, wanting to stay in the South Side is as unthinkable as moving to Edinburgh. The West End, however, as it boasts far more than most other areas the warmth and vitality that have for long been associated with Glasgow, is the part of town most likely to appeal to an outsider who is in the city for a few days.

GREENBANK GARDEN
Eastwood, Strathclyde

Flenders Road, Eastwood, 6m S of Glasgow city centre. All year. Daily 0930–sunset. D. Free. NTS (041–639 3281).

The 2½-acre garden stands primarily as a role-model for private gardeners in the area, demonstrating the range of plants which can be grown in what is reputedly a difficult climate.

GREENOCK
Strathclyde

On A8 23m NW of Glasgow.

Flanked by **Gourock** and Port Glasgow, Greenock has long been one of the most important ports on the **River Clyde**, although the decline of **shipbuilding** in recent decades has hit the town hard. The Maclean Museum and Art Gallery in Union Street includes exhibitions about its history, and about the life of James Watt, inventor of the steam engine, who was born in the town. The Nelson Street cemetery contains the grave of Highland Mary, one of the great loves of **Robert Burns**.

GRETNA GREEN
Dumfries and Galloway

Off A74 at Scotland–England Border.

Although the disparity between Scots and English marriage law is not as wide as once it was, Gretna retains its fame as *the* destination for eloping would-be-weds from south of the Border: in Scotland you can marry at 16 without parental consent. The registrar's office in the village is still very popular, and displays letters of thanks from newly-weds. The Old Blacksmith's Shop Visitor Centre houses a museum, whose exhibits include the anvil which served as a makeshift altar.

GREY MARE'S TAIL
Dumfries and Galloway

Off A708 10m NE of Moffat. All year. Free. NTS (041–552 8391).

High in the hills of the 2410-acre estate, purchased by the National Trust for Scotland in 1962, this 200-foot-high waterfall is one of the most spectacular, and best known, in the country. The area contains a wealth of wildflowers, and a herd of wild goats. It is extremely inadvisable to wander from the path, for a number of accidents have occurred in the vicinity.

HAMILTON
Strathclyde

Off M74 15m SE of Glasgow.

Once the centre of the Lanarkshire coalfield, Hamilton was named after the ducal family who latterly lived at nearby **Chatelherault**. Hamilton Old Parish Church was, like Chatelherault, designed by William Adam, and is still used as a place of worship. The grand, gloomy Hamilton Mausoleum in Strathclyde Park was built by the 10th Duke, Alexander, to house his ancestors.

HELENSBURGH
Strathclyde

On N side of Firth of Clyde, facing Greenock.

Sheltered and peaceful, with good leisure facilities and within easy reach of **Glasgow**, Helensburgh was long a favourite venue for the city's business classes, either to live or holiday in; it retains a certain air of respectability today. The town is one of the best venues on the Clyde for cruising and sailing: cruises leave regularly in summer for such destinations as **Bute, Dunoon** and **Gourock**. The most remarkable building in town is the **Hill House**.

HILL HOUSE
Helensburgh, Strathclyde

Upper Colquhoun Street, Helensburgh. 1 April–23 December. Daily 1300–1700. D (P). NTS (0346 73900).

Commissioned in 1902 by Walter Blackie the publisher, and completed two years later, the Hill House is the finest example of **Charles Rennie Mackintosh**'s domestic architecture. Each element in the building contributes to a harmonious whole; even the original garden shed, now disused, is turret-shaped. The interior is preserved as it was when the house was lived in, with Mackintosh's original furniture.

HOLY ISLAND
Strathclyde

Off Arran, 2m SE of Lamlash.

A small island in the Firth of Clyde just off **Arran**, Holy Island is currently off-limits to the public. It was bought by Buddhist monks in November 1991 for a sum below the asking price of £1 million. Their plans for the island include the development of a religious retreat for use by people of all faiths, the restoration of a ruined chapel and the creation of a nature reserve. Their **Kagyu Samye Ling** monastery near Eskdalemuir is open to the public.

HUNTERSTON POWER STATION
near Largs, Strathclyde

By A78 5m S of Largs. All year. Daily. Phone to arrange guided tour. D. Free (0800 838557 (free) or 0294 822311).

Now owned by Scottish Nuclear, Hunterston produces up to a quarter of all electricity consumed in Scotland. Hunterston A, a Magnox reactor, was opened in 1964; from then until 1980 it was assessed as the best performing nuclear power station in the world.

Its shutdown programme began in
1988. Hunterston B, an advanced
gas-cooled reactor, was opened
in the mid 1970s. The new visitor
centre at the station includes an
exhibition about Hunterston and the
nuclear industry. The guided tour
of the station takes visitors round
viewing galleries which look on to
the turbine hall, the central control
room, and the reactor hall.

INVERARAY
Strathclyde

On A83, on NW shore of Loch Fyne.

A popular, picturesque tourist centre, Inveraray as it currently stands is an 18th-century creation, the impetus for expansion coming from the construction by the 3rd Duke of Argyll of a new **Inveraray Castle**. The original castle was built in 1415, but three centuries later had become dilapidated, prompting the duke to build a new home. Between 1743 and 1765 the old town which was based around the old castle disappeared, to be replaced by the current, carefully laid-out town half a mile to the south – thus putting some space between the locals and the duke and his family. **Inveraray Jail** in the town centre is now a museum. The granite bell-tower in the Episcopal Church of All Saints houses the world's second heaviest ring of ten bells. In the summer months, the MV *Rover* departs from Inveraray pier hourly to tour Loch Fyne.

INVERARAY CASTLE AND GARDENS
Inveraray, Strathclyde

½m N of Inveraray. Jul–Aug, Mon–Sat 1000–1730, Sun 1300–1730; Apr–Jun, Sept–mid Oct, Mon–Thurs, Sat 1000–1230, 1400–1730, Sun 1300–1730. D (P) (0499 2203).

A splendid neo-Gothic affair – not at all what one would expect to find on the southern fringes of the Highlands – Inveraray Castle was built by the Duke of Argyll in the mid 18th century. Roger Morris began work in 1743, and later the Adam family of architects were involved in the construction. The castle houses a fine collection of portraits, including works by Gainsborough, Raeburn and Ramsay. The gardens are open by appointment.

INVERARAY JAIL
Inveraray, Strathclyde

In centre of Inveraray. All year. Daily 0930–1700. D (P) (0499 2381).

Once the site of draconian sentences, including deportation to Australia, Inveraray Jail is now a museum, where ostensible 19th-century prisoners guide visitors round such exhibits as the whipping machine and the 1820 courtroom, now peopled by dummies.

INVERAWE SMOKERY AND FISHERIES
Strathclyde

On A85 NW of Loch Awe. Smokehouses all year, daily 0900–1700. Fisheries Apr–Oct 0900–1800. D (P). Free (08662 446).

The Inverawe Smokery and Fisheries provide a chance to learn about the traditional methods of smoking and curing fish, and to see the raw material – the fish are stocked in three lochs which are used for angling.

IONA, ISLE OF
Strathclyde

Off SW tip of Mull. All year. Daily. Abbey gift/bookshop: Mon–Sat 1000–1700, Sun 1200–1700. Abbey coffee house: Mar–Oct,

Mon–Sat 1100–1630, Sun 1200–1600. D
(P). Free. NTS (06817 404).

The ferry from Fionnphort on **Mull**
takes you to the small island where,
in 563, St Columba and a handful
of followers founded a monastery.
A new monastery was built early
in the 13th century, but it and the
cathedral were dilapidated for
centuries, before, in 1938, George
Macleod, later Lord Macleod of
Fuinary, established a new Christian
community on the island. Iona was,
however, a place of pilgrimage long
before the present community was
established; Samuel Johnson, for
instance, visited the island on his
tour of the Western Isles in 1773.
The oldest building now standing is
the restored St Oran's Chapel, which
dates from 1080; Scottish kings,
Duncan and Macbeth among them,
are buried in its cemetery. For many
visitors this is a much-loved spot, a
place whose tranquillity renders it
ideal for contemplation; conversely,
more robust, active visitors may
wish to escape the odour of sanctity
after a while. The latter are advised
to go beyond the eastern shore,
where the religious buildings are
concentrated, and explore the
beaches to the north, or the boggy
country to the south. Most of the
island – with the exception of
the cathedral and other sacred or
historic buildings – is in the care
of the National Trust for Scotland.
Cruises run from Iona to **Staffa**.

IRVINE
Strathclyde

On A78 6m W of Kilmarnock.

Once a thriving commercial port,
the New Town of Irvine now caters
for holidaymakers. The Scottish

Maritime Museum in Harbourside
records the life in centuries past of
sailors and shipyard workers, and
includes several working boats.

ISLAY, ISLE OF
Strathclyde

W of Kintyre peninsula.

Separated from **Jura** only by a
narrow stretch of water, Islay
(pronounced ile–a, that is, without
the 'y') is accessible by ferry from
Kennacraig in Kintyre. About
25 miles long by 20 wide, the
island was originally ruled by the
Norsemen, and then by the Lord of
the Isles, whose council meetings
were held in Islay's **Finlaggan Castle**.
Although the population has slowly
dwindled – at several thousand
it is less than a quarter of what it
was at its peak last century – the
economy of the island is now on a
stable footing, its mainstays being
whisky, tourism and agriculture.
The Museum of Islay Life in Port
Charlotte records the island's history
from earliest times to the present
day. In Kildalton churchyard,
seven miles east of Port Ellen, the
Kildalton cross is among the best
examples of Celtic crosses to be
found anywhere in Scotland. Islay is
renowned for its malt whisky: you
can tour the distillery in the village
of **Bowmore**, and Laphroaig distillery
in Port Ellen.

ISLAY, BOWMORE

14m N of Port Ellen.

The seat of the old Islay parliament
between 1718 and 1843, the village
of Bowmore boasts what is said

to be the oldest legal distillery on the island (guided tours may be arranged). Bowmore Round Church, also known as Kilarrow Parish Church, was built in 1769, and is probably a copy of an Italian design. Its shape – round – is said to have been decided upon because of the superstition that evil spirits need corners to hide in.

ISLAY, FINLAGGAN CASTLE

On an islet in Loch Finlaggan.

Now a ruin, Finlaggan Castle was the seat of the Lords of the Isles who ruled Islay in the Middle Ages. Fiercely independent of – and sometimes in armed conflict with – the Scottish crown, the lords held their council meetings at Finlaggan, deciding policy and adjudicating disputes between their subjects.

JURA, ISLE OF
Strathclyde

W of Kintyre peninsula.

A rough, rugged island, Jura is far more sparsely inhabited than its westerly neighbour **Islay**. Around 200 people live on the island, mainly on the sheltered eastern coast; reached only from Islay, and with only one road, Jura is likely to appeal to the more ascetically inclined visitor. One such was George Orwell, who wrote *Nineteen Eighty-Four* on the island when he was already suffering from the tuberculosis which brought about his early death. The principal attractions for visitors are climbing – on the dramatic Paps of Jura in the south – rambling and birdwatching.

KAGYU SAMYE LING TIBETAN MONASTERY
Dumfries and Galloway

On B709 N of Eskdalemuir. All year. Daily. D (P). Free.

The only Buddhist monastery in Scotland offers guided tours to visitors. Buddhism and the Borders may sound an unlikely combination, but the traditional buildings blend in very well with the surrounding countryside. The Buddhist monks have recently bought **Holy Island**.

KEIL
Strathclyde

W of Southend, on Kintyre peninsula.

Keil is reputedly the site of St Columba's first landing in Scotland; a flat rock marks the spot.

KELBURN COUNTRY CENTRE
Strathclyde

Off A78, between Largs and Fairlie. Easter–mid Oct, daily 1000–1800. Castle late April–late May, daily 1200–1600. D (P) (0475 568685).

Home of the Earls of Glasgow, Kelburn, when weather permits, has breathtaking views out to the islands of **Cumbrae, Bute** and **Arran**. Kelburn Glen itself is a well-known beauty spot, while the gardens around the castle contain such rarities as 1000-year-old yew trees. There are many activities for children, including pony-trekking, a nature centre, and – for robust adults as well – a commando course.

KENMURE CASTLE
Dumfries and Galloway

Off A762 1m S of New Galloway.

A 16th-century ruin, accessible only on foot, Kenmure was home to the Gordons of Lochinvar, who provided a safe haven for Mary Queen of Scots when she was escaping to England.

KILBERRY SCULPTURED STONES
Strathclyde

Off B8024 20m SW of Lochgilphead. All year. Daily. Free. HS (031–244 3101).

This site is a notable collection of sculptured stones from the late Middle Ages.

KILLIN
Central

On A827 7m N of Lochearnhead.

In the former Breadalbane estate, on the northern border with Tayside Region, Killin is a picturesque, welcoming village spliced by the dramatic Falls of Dochart and the River Dochart. Altogether less welcoming is Finlarig Castle half a mile to the north, the stark, ruined home of a branch of Clan Campbell.

KILMARNOCK
Strathclyde

On A71 7m E of Irvine.

In common with many other Ayrshire towns and villages,

Kilmarnock has strong connections with poet **Robert Burns**; most famously, it lent its name to the 1786 edition of his poems, the success of which persuaded him against emigrating to Jamaica. The Burns Monument and Museum in Kay Park, which contains a statue of the poet sculpted by W.G. Stevenson, is closed to the public. The Dick Institute in Elmbank Avenue combines a museum, with exhibitions on, among other subjects, local and natural history, and an art gallery, which features touring exhibitions. Whisky is the town's most important industry; the Johnnie Walker distillery in Hill Street offers free tours on weekdays. **Dean Castle** is set in a 200-acre country park. The novels *Docherty* and *The Big Man* by William McIlvanney are set in 'Graithnock', a lightly fictionalized version of Kilmarnock.

KILMARTIN SCULPTURED STONES
Strathclyde

On A816, 7½m N of Lochgilphead. All year. Daily. Free (031–244 3101).

Situated in an area rich in relics both ancient and medieval, this churchyard contains a number of well-preserved locally carved gravestones, as well as fragments of two crosses.

KILPATRICK, OLD
Strathclyde

On A814 2m W of the Erskine Bridge.

Despite the fact that *Kil* means burial place, this is reputed to be

the birthplace of the patron saint of Ireland. It is probably the etymology that is wrong rather than the folk memory: while it is universally accepted that Patrick was buried in his adopted land, the available evidence – although not proving his place of birth – does show that it was from around this area that he was captured as a young man and taken to Ireland.

KILWINNING
Strathclyde

On A737 3m E of Saltcoats.

Kilwinning is generally regarded as the birthplace in Scotland of freemasonry, a fact which is recognized by the honorific title 'Mother Kilwinning' to describe the town's own lodge. The craft claims its roots go back to ancient times, but in this country at least it seems to have derived from the guild of stonemasons; those working on Kilwinning Abbey, begun in the 12th century and now a ruin, are reputed to have originated the secret society in 1107. The abbey was built on the site of the eighth-century Church of St Winnen, from which Kilwinning (*kil* meaning burial place) takes its name. **Dalgarven Mill** in Dalry Road is an agricultural and costume museum.

KIPPEN
Central

On A811 6m W of Stirling.

A small village just to the south of the River Forth, Kippen was once made a kingdom in its own right, to prevent the acquisition of land by

King James IV. One villager, John Buchanan, was later declared King of Kippen by James V. Being north of the Highland Line, Kippen was exempt from the whisky tax, and consequently boasted a number of distilleries. It was not, however, exempt from other vicissitudes: **Rob Roy Macgregor** clashed with the men of Kippen while attempting a raid on a cattle herd being driven from **Menteith** to **Stirling**. The heart of the village is the Kippen Smiddy, owned by the National Trust for Scotland; it was occupied by the same family of blacksmiths from 1721 until 1986. As it is still a working smiddy, the building is not generally open to the public, although open days are advertised from time to time.

KIRKCUDBRIGHT
Dumfries and Galloway

Off A75 15m SW of Dumfries.

Standing at the mouth of the River Dee, Kirkcudbright (pronounced Kir-coo-bry) is one of the most pleasant towns in the south of the country, and enjoys a mild climate.

The harbour, with its colourful houses, has long been a favourite spot for artists. MacLellan's Castle just off the High Street dates from 1577, although it has been ruined since the mid 18th century. The Stewartry Museum in St Mary Street documents the life of the area. Nearby **Tongland Power Station** can be visited.

KIRTLEBRIDGE
Dumfries and Galloway

Off A74 6m NE of Annan.

Not far from the Border with England, Kirtlebridge is the site of the nine-foot-high Merkland Cross, raised in the 14th century in memory of one of the famous Maxwell family. The Clydesdale Horse Centre at nearby Robgill Tower is home to workhorses; exhibits include the harnesses and other equipment used.

LADY ROCK
Strathclyde

Off Lismore Lighthouse at the head of Loch Linnhe.

The boat from **Oban** to **Mull** passes Lady Rock, the spot where the wife of one of the Maclean family was dumped by her husband. Rescued by fishermen, she was returned to her father, a Campbell, who, as retribution, killed her husband.

LAKE OF MENTEITH
Central

Off A81 3m E of Aberfoyle.

The only Scottish body of water to be known as a lake – all the others, of course, are lochs – the Lake of Menteith was originally known as the Loch of Inchmahome, before a confusion with the word *laigh* – Scots for low-lying ground, a term which was applied to the whole area – gave it its present name. The lake is one of the best-known fly-fishing centres in the country, and is host to a wide range of birds. When weather permits – which is once a decade at best – it is also the venue for a curling bonspiel, or competition, in which teams from all over Scotland take part. Inchmahome Priory, on the largest of the lake's three islands, was founded in 1238 for an Augustinian community, and was used as a refuge for Mary Queen of Scots in 1547, after an English army had invaded Scotland. Though ruined, the buildings are the best preserved of their kind in the country, and still give a good idea of what medieval monastic life was like.

LANARK
Strathclyde

On A73 14m SE of Hamilton.

One of the few centres of population of any size in the area not to be dominated by heavy industry, Lanark is a relatively quiet market town. On the main street, the statue of William Wallace in a niche in the church tower commemorates the man who began the **Wars of Independence**. In 1297, after his wife was murdered by the English, Wallace burnt the town and killed the English sheriff before retreating to the forest of Selkirk to regroup and begin his guerrilla campaign. Lanimer Day, a festive occasion equivalent to the Border Ridings, is celebrated every June. A mile south of the town are **New Lanark** and the Falls of Clyde.

LAND O'BURNS CENTRE
Alloway, Strathclyde

In Murdoch's Lone. All year. Daily. Spring, June and autumn 1000–1730; July, Aug 1000–1800, winter 1000–1700. D. Free (0292 43700).

The Land O' Burns Centre is a visitor centre devoted to poet **Robert Burns**. Not as atmospheric as the other sites on the Burns Heritage Trail which runs through **Alloway**, the centre may prove too kitsch for some tastes. It does, however, offer an audio-visual presentation, for which there is a small charge, about Burns and his verse.

LANGHOLM
Dumfries and Galloway

On A7 9m N of Scotland–England Border.

On the eastern edge of Dumfries
and Galloway, this mill town,
where the Esk meets the Ewes,
seems more akin to the towns of
Borders Region than it does to those
further west, especially given the
importance of rugby in Langholm
life. The Common Riding, one of
the annual festivals which take
place throughout the Borders, takes
place every July, and for a day it
seems as if the whole town is on
horseback. The Hugh MacDiarmid
monument, at Whita Hill Yett, two
miles north-east of the town on the
Newcastleton road, is a sculpture
by Jake Harvey commemorating
the Langholm-born leader of the
Scots literary renaissance. Two
miles north-east, the Craigcleuch
Collection is a gathering of
ethnographical objects from around
the world. Seven miles south of the
town, off the A7, is Scots Dyke,
the remains of a wall which once
marked the Border with England.

LARGS
Strathclyde

On A78 on Clyde coast, opposite Cumbrae.

One of many holiday resorts on the
Clyde coast, Largs has the usual
panoply of golf courses, swimming
pools and other leisure facilities,
such as Kelburn Country Centre
just south of the town on the road
to Fairlie. The Battle of Largs in
1263, fought by the Norwegians
and the Scots in a dispute over the
Western Isles, is commemorated
annually, when locals dress up as
the opposing armies and parade
through the town. Largs Museum
in Manse Court celebrates this and
other events in local history. Ferries
make the short journey to Cumbrae
from Largs.

LEADHILLS
Strathclyde

On B797 18m S of Lanark.

Leadhills was the birthplace of the
poet Allan Ramsay (1686–1758),
whose father was manager of the
lead mines which gave the village
its name. The Allan Ramsay Library
was founded by the poet in 1741 as
a subscription library, and contains
local records, foremost among them
being documents of the lead-mining
industry. The nearby village of
Wanlockhead claims to be the highest
village in Scotland.

LEGLEN WOOD
Strathclyde

4m E of Ayr.

An attractive spot above the River
Ayr, Leglen Wood was often
visited by Robert Burns; a cairn
and inscription now mark his
favourite spot.

LINCLUDEN COLLEGIATE CHURCH
Dumfries and Galloway

Off A76 1m N of Dumfries.
Apr–Sept, Mon–Sat 0930–1900, Sun
1400–1900; Oct–Mar, Mon–Wed, Sat,
0930–1600, Thurs 0930–1300, Sun
1400–1600. HS (031–244 3101).

Built in the 15th century – although
the original building on the
site, for Benedictine nuns, was
constructed in the 12th century –
the church includes the tomb of
Princess Margaret, daughter of King
Robert III.

LISMORE ISLAND
Strathclyde

On Loch Linnhe 6m N of Oban.

Accessible by ferry from **Oban**, long, thin Lismore Island was once home to the Bishop of Argyll, whose 13th-century Achanduin Castle, now ruined, stands in the south-west.

DAVID LIVINGSTONE CENTRE
Blantyre, Strathclyde

On A725 8m SE of Glasgow. Early Mar–end Oct (other times by arrangement), Mon–Sat 1000–1800, Sun 1400–1800. D (P) (0698 823140).

Based around the tenement where the missionary and explorer David Livingstone (1813–73) was born, the centre commemorates the first European to discover Victoria Falls, who had a famous meeting with H.M. Stanley, and died while searching for the source of the Nile. The conditions of Livingstone's early life in Scotland are recalled in the tenement itself, now a museum, while his connection with Africa – where, as well as exploration, he did much to expose and undermine the slave trade – is highlighted by the African Pavilion, which houses exhibitions pertaining to life in the continent today.

LOCHEARNHEAD
Central

On A85 14m N of Callander.

On the western edge of the loch, this holiday village has a popular watersports centre, which hires equipment and offers tuition in water-skiing, windsurfing, and others. A pleasant woodland walk takes you up the glen to the Falls of Edinample.

LOCHGILPHEAD
Strathclyde

On A83 24m SW of Inveraray.

The southern end of the Crinan Canal, the small market town of Lochgilphead looks out on to Loch Fyne. Formerly an important herring port, it is now the main shopping centre for the area, and is an increasingly popular holiday resort. In clement weather, the hills of **Arran** can be seen off to the south.

LOCH KEN
Dumfries and Galloway

Alongside A713 S of New Galloway.

Fed by the Black Water of Dee in the west, this narrow 10-mile-long loch attracts anglers and watersports enthusiasts during the spring and summer months, and birdwatchers throughout the year, particularly to see greylag and whitefront geese in the winter. The southern shores are well-wooded and to the north-west is the ruined **Kenmure Castle**.

LOCH LOMOND, see panel p130.

LOCHMABEN
Dumfries and Galloway

On A709 9m NE of Dumfries.

Loch Lomond

T he largest, best-known, and most romantic of Scotland's lochs, Loch Lomond is 23 miles long and, at its widest point, five miles across. From **Balloch** at its southern tip to Tarbet and Inversnaid on its northern shores, Loch Lomond is almost conventionally beautiful, so familiar are the images that the visitor finds here. The Highland Boundary Fault, the geological feature which separates Scotland's Highlands from Lowlands, lies underneath the loch; thus the land surrounding the southern shores is flatter and less formidable, but further north the hills get higher. At 3194 feet, Ben Lomond, north of **Rowardennan**, is Scotland's southernmost Munro, mountain over 3000 feet are known.

The beauty of the area and the ease with which it is reached – there is a fast, regular train service to Balloch from **Glasgow** – has ensured that Loch Lomond is now one of Britain's busiest stretches of water, to the extent that the environment is threatened. Water-skiing and the use of motor boats, particularly popular at the Balloch end, may be merely a nuisance to those who prefer relaxation to such robust activities, but the waterway is now so congested that accidents are becoming increasingly common. A wide range of leisure pursuits is on offer: there are daily cruises in season; there are many fine areas for fishing (the British record for a pike – 47lb 10oz – was from Loch Lomond); while Balloch Castle Country Park, and Queen Elizabeth National Forest Park to the east of Rowardennan, both offer a chance to find a more peaceful spot for a picnic or a long walk. There are 37 islands on the loch, the largest being Inchmurrin, which has a hotel. There is a nature reserve on Inchcailloch; while **Bucinch and Ceardach** are owned by the National Trust for Scotland. Several of the villages around the loch are a riot of floral colour in summer; the conservation village of **Luss** is the setting for Scottish Television's soap opera *Take The High Road* – and it is well worth visiting – while, on the quieter eastern shore, Drymen includes the historic spot where **Rob Roy Macgregor** once collected his protection money.

One of three places which claim to be the birthplace of Robert the Bruce – the others are **Turnberry** and Essex – Lochmaben commemorates its most famous son with a statue on the main road. Lochmaben Castle, on the south shore of Castle Loch, was a favourite spot for James IV.

LOCKERBIE
Dumfries and Galloway

Off A74 10m N of Annan.

Once known only as a thriving market town, Lockerbie is now remembered as the site of the disaster in December 1988 in which, a bomb having been planted on board, a Pan Am jet exploded over the town, killing all the passengers and, crashing on to a residential street, some of the residents as well. Lockerbie's lamb fairs and the produce of the surrounding farms are still the most important economic activities for the town. Cumstone Farm in nearby Corrie offers buggy trails, suitable for adults and children, through an area which has good views of **Burnswark** and the Annan valley.

LOGAN BOTANIC GARDEN
Dumfries and Galloway

On the B7065 14m S of Stranraer.
Mar–Oct, daily 1000–1800. D (P)
(077 686 231).

A branch of Edinburgh's Royal Botanic Garden, the Logan Gardens take advantage of the mild south-western climate to cultivate many sub-tropical species. The nearby Logan Fish Pond – really a rock pool – was completed in 1800, and was originally used as a stock of live fish for Logan House. It is now home to around 30 tame trout.

LUSS
Strathclyde

On A82 8m NE of Helensburgh.

On the western shore of **Loch Lomond**, Luss is a conservation village, and a delightful place to visit in summer, when the flowers grown in each cottage garden are in bloom. Many tourists, however, visit Luss principally because it is the setting for the Scottish Television soap opera *Take the High Road*. Art has imitated reality to the extent that members of the cast can often be seen conducting tour groups around 'their' village.

HUGH MACDIARMID, see
panel p133.

MACEACHIN'S CAVE
Central

On A977 by Rumbling Bridge.

This was the hideout after the 1746 Battle of Culloden of Hector Maceachin, a Jacobite who escaped from **Castle Campbell**. The woman who helped hide him, Hannah Haig, later became his wife.

ROB ROY MACGREGOR, see
panel p134.

MACHRIHANISH
Strathclyde

On B843 6m W of Campbeltown.

On the western side of the Kintyre peninsula, and hence far more exposed than *Campbeltown* to the east, Machrihanish is, none the less, a popular holiday resort, its remoteness adding to its appeal.

CHARLES RENNIE
MACKINTOSH, see panel p135.

MAUCHLINE
Strathclyde

On A758 11m NE of Ayr.

After **Alloway**, the poet's birthplace, Mauchline is one of the most important stops on the **Robert Burns** trail. The National Burns Memorial Tower was opened in 1896, and now contains a visitor centre on the first two floors, with a viewing area at the top of the tower. Poosie Nansie's pub, which features in Burns's cantata *The Jolly Beggars*, still performs its original function today. Highland Mary's monument, three miles west of Mauchline at Failford, marks the place where, it is said, Burns parted from Mary Campbell, one of his sweethearts, in 1786.

MAYBOLE COLLEGIATE
CHURCH
Strathclyde

In Maybole, 8m SW of Ayr. Free. HS (031–244 3101).

Now viewable from the outside only, this is the roofless ruin of a 15th-century church, built by the Kennedys of Dunure.

MENSTRIE
Central

On A91 5m NE of Stirling.

The westernmost of the Hillfoots villages, Menstrie, in common with its neighbours, has a long tradition as a centre for the milling industry. **Menstrie Castle** is managed by the National Trust for Scotland.

Hugh MacDiarmid

Born **as Christopher Murray Grieve in Langholm**, Hugh MacDiarmid (1892–1978) is considered by many to be the most important Scottish poet of the century, having led the Scottish literary renaissance of the inter-war years. He served with the medical corps in World War I, and was a journalist in Montrose in the 1920s before bursting on to the literary scene in 1926 with *A Drunk Man Looks at the Thistle*, a complex examination of the Scottish psyche. A committed communist and Scottish nationalist (he was a founder member of the National Party of Scotland), he experienced no difficulty in reconciling these two strands of his politics, but was expelled from both parties at different times. Despite his avowed allegiance to the working class, he was never able to adopt the popular touch successfully: standing for election under his real name, he employed the slogan 'Honour Scotland, honour yourself, vote Grieve'. His politics were much in evidence in his later work, which included the two *Hymns to Lenin*, and *On A Raised Beach*.

The bulk of his poetry was written in a hybrid Scots dialect, with words drawn from the town and country, north and south, rural areas and the cities. The magnitude of his achievement is undeniable, yet the fact that virtually every Scot today would need a glossary to understand his work suggests that, in years to come, the influence of MacDiarmid's work – its form if not necessarily its content – will diminish, and may even come to be regarded as a glorious irrelevance.

A profound if unsystematic thinker, MacDiarmid was a mass of contradictions. From the end of World War II until his death he lived in a cottage just outside **Biggar**. He was little honoured in his home town of Langholm, and after his death an unseemly dispute arose when planning permission for a memorial to him was at first refused. Eventually, though, a sculpture was erected at Whita Hill Yett, two miles north-east of the town.

Rob Roy Macgregor

Born near **Balquhidder** into a family that had been out-lawed for a century, Rob Roy (1671–1734), soon to become famous as a cattle rustler, was initially himself a victim of the rustlers, and is said only to have taken up arms to protect himself and his family. Espousing the Jacobite cause (the claim to the throne by the Stuarts), he began rustling in 1691, and two or three years later claimed the title of clan chief. His lands were seized in 1712 when he lost heavily on cattle speculation and was unable to repay loans from the Duke of Montrose. His wife and children having been turned out of their home in midwinter, Rob Roy declared war on the duke. The legend of the Gregor chief as a latterday Robin Hood, who would plunder the baggage trains of the Scottish aristocracy and distribute the takings among the rural poor, began to grow around this time, although there is evidence to suggest that it was often ordinary cattle-farmers who were the victims of Rob Roy's raids. The men of **Kippen**, for instance, clashed with Rob Roy's forces when the latter attempted a raid on a herd being driven from **Menteith** to **Stirling**. Eventually arrested in 1727, he was sentenced to transportation, but was pardoned. After a wild, often violent life, he died peacefully, in bed, in Balquhidder, and is buried, along with his wife and two of their sons, in the village churchyard. Sir Walter Scott's novel *Rob Roy* is a romanticized picture of the man. The Rob Roy and Trossachs Visitor Centre in **Callander** gives more information on his life and times.

Charles Rennie Mackintosh

Born in **Glasgow**, the multi-talented Charles Rennie Mackintosh (1868–1928) is principally remembered now as the most influential Scottish architect of modern times, but he was also an outstanding graphic designer and water-colourist, and the inventor of a distinctive elongated typeface which, during Glasgow's year as European Capital of Culture in 1990, was used on everything from T-shirts to official press releases. His architectural output was not large, but was extremely influential. The **Glasgow School of Art** (1897–1909) is generally regarded as his masterpiece. Other significant works are the **Hill House**, **Helensburgh** and Glasgow's **Scotland Street School**, while examples of his work can be seen at the Mackintosh House in the **Hunterian Art Gallery**, and the Willow Tea Rooms in Sauchiehall Street, both in Glasgow.

Mackintosh would design a building down to the smallest piece of furniture it was due to contain, making for a harmonious whole. The strong external lines of such buildings as the Hill House are a distinct contrast to the soft, almost sentimental, furnishings, partly inspired by the Celtic Twilight movement which was in vogue at the time.

An artist without honour in his own country, he left Scotland in 1914, and largely abandoned architecture in favour of painting. In his last years, while in France, he produced a series of celebrated watercolours. While conventional bourgeois taste in Britain found Mackintosh's blend of the ultra-modern with hints of medievalism to be too outré and experimental, he was regarded in the opposite light by many critics on the Continent: at a time when mechanical brutalism was coming into fashion, Mackintosh's output was regarded as recherché, a hopelessly sentimental attempt to return to a romanticized version of the past. None the less, he was acclaimed in Austria and Germany at the beginning of the century, and few would now contest his genius. Overexposed he may have been in recent years – at least in the city of his birth, where a welter of 'Mockintosh' material awaits the unsuspecting tourist – but a visit to his best buildings is a reminder of his inspired originality.

MENSTRIE CASTLE
Menstrie, Central

In Menstrie, 5m NE of Stirling. Open by arrangement with National Trust for Scotland's Perth office (0738 31296).

Menstrie Castle is a restored 16th-century building which now stands in the middle of a housing scheme. Sir William Alexander, King James VI's Lieutenant for Nova Scotia, was born here, and one of the rooms is given over to a display of the coats of arms of Nova Scotian baronetcies.

THE MILL ON THE FLEET
Gatehouse of Fleet, Dumfries and Galloway

In Gatehouse of Fleet town centre. Mar–Nov, daily 1000–1800; phone for winter times. D (0557 814099).

The Mill on the Fleet celebrates the past and present of the attractive town of **Gatehouse of Fleet**. Visitors can see the designing and building of Cally House, the home of the local laird, James Murray, who established the town and its industry, while in the centre's auditorium an audio-visual presentation gives a buzzard's-eye view of rural Galloway.

MILNGAVIE
Strathclyde

8m NW of Glasgow city centre.

An affluent suburb just outside the city boundary, Milngavie (pronounced 'Mullguy') is the starting point of the **West Highland Way**; would-be walkers are advised

always to travel the route from south to north, as the relative ease of the southern sections allows 'acclimatization'. The Heatherbank Museum and Library of Social Work Trust, in Mugdock Road, is the only social work museum in Europe, with a reference library, archive collection, and exhibition room.

MOFFAT
Dumfries and Galloway

Off A74 15m N of Lockerbie.

Moffat's long history as a sheep-farming centre is marked by the Moffat Ram, a large bronze statue which stands at one end of the High Street. It was in Moffat, in 1795, that the young James Macpherson first made public his 'translations' of the works of Ossian, said to be an ancient Gaelic poet. The consensus now is that, although snatches may have come from Highland oral tradition, the bulk of Macpherson's revelations were his own creation. A well-kept and pleasant town, Moffat was once a popular spa; the surrounding countryside is ideal for walking. The picturesque **Devil's Beef Tub** lies six miles to the north.

MONIAIVE
Dumfries and Galloway

On B729 15m NW of Dumfries.

A pleasantly situated village, Moniaive contains a memorial to James Renwick, one of the most famous Covenanters, who was born in the village in 1662, proclaimed the **Lanark** and **Sanquhar** Declarations, and was captured and killed in Edinburgh in 1688. Three miles to the south-west on the B729, just past Kirkland, lies the 14th-century Maxwelton House, home to the Laurie family, among them Annie Laurie (fl. early 18th century), remembered in a traditional Scots song named after her.

MOTHERWELL
Strathclyde

On A721 15m SE of Glasgow.

In the depressed heartland of the central belt, Motherwell is home to the giant Ravenscraig steel works, the closure of which, for long expected, was finally announced in January 1992. While EC or central government funding may be forthcoming, the outlook for the Motherwell area seems bleak for some time to come.

MOTTE OF URR
near Dalbeattie, Dumfries and Galloway

On B794 2m NW of Dalbeattie.

Built in the 12th century, the Motte of Urr is the largest motte and bailey castle in the country. Its central mound is 80 feet high. Six miles to the south lies **Orchardton Tower**.

MULL, ISLE OF
Strathclyde

In Firth of Lorn, W of Oban.

The largest of the Inner Hebrides, Mull is accessible by ferry from **Oban**. The island has seen its population slowly decline over the last two centuries, until now only a couple of thousand people live there. It is a popular island for holidays and short breaks. At Craignure, the ferry's first stopping-off point, you can catch the **Mull and West Highland Narrow Gauge Railway**. The ferry also calls at the capital of Mull, **Tobermory**, in the far north of the island. Other points of interest on the island include **Burg, Dervaig, Duart Castle** and the **Macquarie Mausoleum**.

MULL, BURG

Off B8035 5m W of Tiroran. All year. Free. NTS (041–552 8391).

This property of over 1500 acres on the north shore of Loch Scridain is accessible only via a footpath from Tiroran, the last point where cars are permitted. Beyond Burg farm, MacCulloch's Fossil Tree, estimated to be 50 million years old, can be reached at low water.

MULL, DERVAIG

On B8073 6m W of Tobermory.

Dervaig is home to the smallest professional theatre in the UK, Mull Little Theatre. A mile out of Dervaig on the Torloisk road, the Old Byre is a museum and visitor centre specializing in the fauna of the island. **Staffa** and the **Treshnish Isles** are accessible by boat from Dervaig.

MULL, DUART CASTLE

Off A849 on E point of Mull. May–Sept, daily 1030–1800 (068 02 309).

Overlooking the Sound of Mull, Duart Castle's oldest section, the keep, dates from the 13th century; the building was expanded four centuries later. Originally belonging to the Maclean family, the castle and estates were forfeited during the 1745 Rebellion because of support for the Jacobites, only returning to their original owners in the early years of this century.

MULL, MACQUARIE MAUSOLEUM

In Gruline. Open all year. Free.

Administered by the National Trust for Scotland on behalf of its Australian counterpart, the mausoleum stands in memory of Lachlan Macquarie (1761–1824), who was born at nearby Ulva Ferry, became governor of New South Wales, and was so successful in improving the morale and economy of the colony that he became known as the 'father of Australia'.

MULL, MULL AND WEST HIGHLAND NARROW GAUGE RAILWAY
Craignure to Torosay Castle.

Trains run in conjunction with ferry, Easter, end Apr–mid Oct. Castle:Easter–mid Oct, daily 1030–1730. Gardens: all year, daylight hours (0631 63122).

Opened in 1984, the Mull and West Highland is the only island passenger railway in Scotland. It runs from Craignure, the first stopping-off point for the ferry from **Oban**, to Torosay Castle. Parts of this Scottish baronial building along with the surrounding 12 acres of terraced gardens, are open to the public.

MULL, TOBERMORY

The capital of Mull, Tobermory is a small town of brightly painted stone buildings, situated at the northern end of the Sound of Mull. An increasingly popular holiday destination, Tobermory harbour is packed with visiting yachts in summer. The Mull and **Iona** Museum on Main Street in the town records the history of both islands.

NEW ABBEY
Dumfries and Galloway

On A710 6m S of Dumfries.

Dominated by **Sweetheart Abbey**, the village of New Abbey has an 18th-century corn mill which is still in working order, as is sometimes demonstrated to visitors. The Shambellie House Museum of Costume, surrounded by scenic woodland, has a different display every year loaned by the National Costume Collection.

NEW GALLOWAY
Dumfries and Galloway

On A762 18m N of Kirkcudbright.

Once surrounded by forest, New Galloway now has a hydro-electric development nearby. Begun between the World Wars, it was the first in Scotland. Two miles to the west, the New Galloway Farm Heritage Centre houses Clydesdale horses and agricultural equipment from the days before mechanization. **Kenmure Castle** is nearby.

NEW LANARK
Strathclyde

Off A73 1m S of Lanark. Visitor Centre: all year. Daily 1100–1700. D (0555 61345.)

A collection of mills and houses, New Lanark was one of the earliest attempts anywhere to provide humane working and living conditions for a group of employees. New Lanark was the brainchild of Robert Owen (1771–1858), the son-in-law of the owner David Dale, himself a philanthropic industrialist. As well as providing decent conditions within the cotton mills, Owen provided education for the children of the workers, and strove to inculcate an understanding of the need for thrift and cleanliness. Today's visitor centre, which is housed in restored mill buildings, includes the 'Annie McLeod Experience': as a cart takes you through an audio-visual display, the young girl Annie tells of her working life in the mills. There is also an exhibition area with a working spinning mule.

NEWTON STEWART
Dumfries and Galloway

Off A75 7m N of Wigtown.

An attractive market town on the River Cree, Newton Stewart is an excellent base from which to explore **Galloway Forest Park** to the north. Other attractions for holidaymakers include birdwatching, boating and fishing.

OBAN
Strathclyde

On A816 37m N of Lochgilphead.

With ferries leaving from here for
Lismore and **Mull**, as well as several
other Hebridean isles, Oban can
often seem a bustling transit town,
despite which it retains its original
charm. McCaig's Tower on a hill
overlooking the town is regarded as
a folly, but the motive behind the
construction was far from foolish.
It was an attempt to overcome the
problem of employment and provide
a memorial to the McCaig family.
Oban Distillery in Stafford Street
welcomes visitors, while a more
unusual spot to visit is A World In
Miniature on the North Pier, where
all the exhibitions – the rooms, the
furniture – are one twelfth of life
size. The island of Kerrera, which
lies just off the town in Oban Bay,
is where King Alexander II died of
fever in 1249.

ORCHARDTON TOWER

Off A711 6m SE of Castle Douglas.
Apr–Sept, Mon–Sat 0930–1900, Sun
1400–1900; Oct–Mar, Mon–Sat 0930–1600,
Sun 1400–1600. D. Free. Apply to custodian
at nearby cottage. HS (031–244 3101).

Built around the middle of the 15th
century, Orchardton is the only
example in Scotland of a circular
tower-house.

PAISLEY
Strathclyde

On A737 7m W of Glasgow.

Not exactly the most picturesque of the many towns which surround **Glasgow**, Paisley, the second largest settlement in Strathclyde, did at least give its name to the colourful, swirling pattern still popular on everything from ties to pyjamas. The Museum and Art Gallery in the High Street traces the history of the Paisley pattern, and houses a collection of Paisley shawls. The most impressive building in the town is Paisley Abbey. Founded in 1163 as a monastery for the Cluniac Order, it was almost completely destroyed by command of Edward I of England in 1307, only to be restored following the winning of independence. The tower collapsed in 1545, leaving the choir in ruins, and it was not until 1928 that the whole building was fully restored. Still used as a place of worship, the abbey houses the Barochan Cross, believed to date from the 10th century. The Sma' Shot Cottages in George Place are preserved two-storey 19th-century houses, originally occupied by millworkers. The foundation for the modern law of negligence came about because of a case brought by a Paisley woman in 1928. At the town's Well Meadow Café, she found a dead snail in her ginger beer and sued the manufacturer.

PARKLEA FARM
Strathclyde

Off A8 1m E of Port Glasgow. All year, daily NTS.

This 68-acre site on the south bank of the Clyde is leased to Inverclyde District Council, who use it as a recreation ground.

PENKILL CASTLE
Strathclyde

At Old Dailly, on B734 2½m NE of Girvan. Apr–Sept, by appointment only (046 587 261).

Originally built in the 15th century, Penkill was added to in stages up to Victorian times, and became a favourite haunt of the Pre-Raphaelite school of painters. Its collection of furniture, tapestries and paintings dates mainly from the 17th and 18th centuries.

THE PINEAPPLE
Central

In Dunmore Park, N of Airth 7m E of Stirling. All year, daily 1000–sunset. Free. NTS (031–226 5922).

This 45-foot-high structure, in the shape of a pineapple, seems strange enough now; when built in 1761, at a time when the tropical fruit was hardly known in this country, it must have appeared even stranger. Built by an unknown architect as a garden retreat, it may be viewed from the outside only, but it is also available for short lets as a holiday home.

PORTAVADIE
Strathclyde

Off B8000 2m W of Millhouse on Cowal peninsula.

The site of one of the most ill-fated industrial ventures in recent history, Portavadie was selected as a construction site for oil platforms; the problem was the lack of demand for oil platforms, which meant that in the end none were built there, and the money spent on preparing the dock was, in effect, swept out to sea.

PORT GLASGOW
Strathclyde

On A8 E of Greenock on S bank of Clyde.

Flanking **Greenock** to the east as **Gourock** does to the west, Port Glasgow, as its name suggests, served as a deep-water port for the city as its maritime trade expanded; consequently, the decline of shipbuilding in the 1970s hit the town hard. On the eastern side of Port Glasgow, Newark Castle, its tower dating from the 15th century, its courtyard and hall from the end of the 16th, is an extremely well-preserved example of a turreted mansion house.

PORTPATRICK
Dumfries and Galloway

Off A77 on W coast of the Rhinns of Galloway.

The starting point of the Southern Upland Way, Portpatrick, just over 20 miles from the Irish mainland, derives its name from a visit said to have been paid by the patron saint of Ireland. Once the main port in the area, it proved to be too exposed, and the ferry for Larne in Northern Ireland now leaves from **Stranraer**.

PRESTWICK
Strathclyde

On A79 3m N of Ayr.

For a long time the site of Scotland's only transatlantic airport, Prestwick has seen its existence – and that of many local jobs – threatened by the expansion of Glasgow airport. In common with other holiday resorts on the Firth of **Clyde**, such as **Troon** and **Turnberry**, Prestwick is renowned as a golfing centre. Bruce's Well, behind St Ninian's Church just south of the town, is said to be where the exhausted and thirsty King Robert struck the ground – and struck water. A lazar or leper house was built by the king in thanks (leprosy is believed to have been the disease which killed him, in 1329).

RED CLYDESIDERS, see
panel p144.

RENFREW
Strathclyde

On A8 8m W of Glasgow city centre.

Once a small country town, Renfrew
was the site, in 1164, of a battle in
which King Malcolm IV of Scotland
defeated and killed Somerled,
Lord of the Isles. Renfrew is now
an adjunct of **Paisley**, both towns
having expanded in recent decades.

RHINNS OF GALLOWAY
Dumfries and Galloway

W peninsula of Galloway.

Shaped like a hammerhead, the
Rhinns (or Rinns) of Galloway is
a peninsula which stretches from
Corsewall Point in the north to the
Mull of Galloway on the south.
Stranraer and **Portpatrick** are the main
towns in the area.

RHU
Strathclyde

On A814 1m W of Helensburgh.

In common with its neighbour
Helensburgh, Rhu enjoys a mild
climate, and is largely devoted to
yachting and boating. Landlubbers
in search of relaxation will find the
town's Glenarn Gardens a pleasant
spot to stop and rest.

ROCKCLIFFE
Dumfries and Galloway

*Off A710 7m S of Dalbeattie. All year. Free
(0556 610117).*

A pretty village and bay on the
Solway Firth, in and around which
the National Trust for Scotland owns
several properties. Mote (or Motte)
of Mark is the site of an ancient hill
fort, and overlooks Rough Island, a
bird sanctuary. Visitors are asked to
stay away from the island in May
and June to allow ground-nesting
birds to raise their new chicks
undisturbed. Muckle Lands and
Jubilee Path are over 50 acres of
rough coastline between Rockcliffe
and the village of Kippford, which
can be reached on foot. In Rockcliffe
itself, the house of Auchenvhin is
also a Trust property, but is not
open to the public.

ROUGH CASTLE
Central

*Off B816 6m W of Falkirk. All year, Free
(031–244 2903).*

The best preserved section of the
Antonine Wall, Rough Castle is the
site of one of the forts which were
dotted along the wall. It was also
one of the sites of the former Falkirk
tryst or cattle market.

ROWARDENNAN
Strathclyde

Off A814 on E side of Loch Lomond.

Some of the best views of **Loch
Lomond** are to be found from
Rowardennan, one of the most

The 'Red Clydesiders'

Scotland as a whole has traditionally been to the political left of England, and **Glasgow**, as the city with the largest concentration of the organized working class, has often been romanticized or stigmatized (depending on your political viewpoint) as a hotbed of revolutionary fervour. The period towards the end of, and immediately after, World War I is recognized as the time when far-left politics were at their most influential in the area, although nowadays most historians argue that fully-fledged communism (the Bolsheviks had taken power in Russia in 1917) had no significant influence. The term 'Red Clydeside' was originally used when the shipyard workers of the area, while the war was still on, refused to allow the introduction of cheaper, unskilled labour to the yards. Newspapers sympathetic to the men were banned, and their leaders were jailed. Despite the fact that the men's industrial action was carried out to defend their own position, some regarded it as a serious assault on the state. The Marxist and Scottish nationalist John Maclean, founder of the Scottish Workers Republican Party, was the most influential communist of the time, and tried – without success – to persuade the Trades Council of Glasgow to declare itself a soviet of workers' deputies along Russian lines. The general election of 1918 was a severe defeat for the left. By the next election in 1922, however, their fortunes had improved, and a sizeable group of Labour MPs was elected from Clydeside, once again inaccurately dubbed 'Red Clydesiders'.

The River Clyde

The role of the River Clyde has changed considerably in recent years with the decline of heavy industry. It gave **Glasgow** its status as a major trading port of the British Empire, and gave rise to shipbuilding on a phenomenal scale. Today, it has become almost exclusively recreational rather than industrial, although originally these two functions of the river were linked, as the hundreds of thousands of families who depended on shipbuilding for their livelihoods usually took their holidays on one of the many resorts on the Firth of Clyde. The trip from Glasgow 'doon the watter' during Fair Fortnight, as the city's trades holidays are known, saw the urban hordes descend on such resorts as **Saltcoats**, **Largs** or **Ayr**, where the traditional holiday entertainments awaited them – variety shows, putting greens, bingo halls.

The same journey today is more likely to be made down the electrified railway line – if, that is, it is made at all. The comparative cheapness of foreign travel has greatly reduced the number of people who want to take their holidays so close to home. Consequently, most of the Clyde resorts have broadened their appeal, in the hope of attracting visitors from outwith the west-coast area, as well as holding on to their loyal local custom. From Largs all the way down to **Girvan** is probably the best stretch of golfing country in Scotland, and it includes the renowned courses at **Turnberry** and **Troon**. There are also good sailing facilities in Troon and Ayr. Further north, where the Gare Loch meets the river, **Helensburgh** is a peaceful, relatively up-market location where, on a good day in summer, the sailing boats on the water seem to outnumber the people on the shore.

In Glasgow itself, where the yards that launched some of the world's greatest ships are now almost all quiet, small ships with on-board restaurants take diners up and down the river. A larger vessel, the MV *Waverley*, the last sea-going paddle-steamer in the world, goes on weekend cruises from Glasgow to the open sea, stopping at many of the resorts on the Firth of Clyde. During the week the *Waverley* is based at Ayr.

popular villages on the lochside.
Just inland, the Queen Elizabeth
National Forest Park stretches
almost to **Aberfoyle**. Rowardennan
is on the **West Highland Way** which
at this point has gone almost a third
of its length from **Milngavie** to Fort
William.

ROZELLE PARK AND MACLAURIN ART GALLERY
Ayr, Strathclyde

Ayr. All year. Mon–Sat 1000–1700;
Apr–Oct, Sun 1400–1700. D (P). Free
(0292 45447).

Rozelle Park is a peaceful haven
even at the height of summer, with
a pitch and putt course, a putting
green, a duck pond, and, adjoining
Rozelle House itself, the Maclaurin
Art Gallery, converted from
stables. The gallery houses touring
Arts Council shows, and selling
exhibitions by contemporary local
artists; the house, an 18th-century
mansion, contains local militaria.

RUMBLING BRIDGE
Central

A823 at Rumbling Bridge. All year. D
(P) Free.

Two bridges span the River Devon
at this spot, where a footpath takes
you down to a series of gorges and
waterfalls, including the loud and
powerful Devil's Mill and Cauldron
Linn, both aptly named.

RUTHWELL
Dumfries and Galloway

Off B725 8½m SE of Dumfries.

The stark, carved cross, 18 feet high,
in Ruthwell Church, dates from
the eighth century. Information on
its restoration and on the savings
bank movement can be found in
Ruthwell's Savings Bank Museum,
which, appropriately enough, was
once a bank itself: the two subjects
are combined in the one museum
because the founder of the bank, the
Rev Dr Henry Duncan, was the man
chiefly responsible for the restoration
of the cross. Brow Well a mile west
of Ruthwell is an old mineral well
which **Robert Burns**, who suffered
from rheumatism, visited on doctor's
orders in 1796, the year of his death.

SADDELL ABBEY
Strathclyde

On B842 9m NW of Campbeltown. All year. Daily. Free.

This 12th-century abbey, built by either Somerled, Lord of the Isles, or his son Reginald, has long been open to the elements. The most impressive feature of the remains are the carved tombstones.

SALTCOATS
Strathclyde

On A78 3m W of Kilwinning.

Contiguous to **Ardrossan**, Saltcoats has long been one of the most popular holiday destinations during the Glasgow Fair, the traditional holiday fortnight for the city's trades. The ease of foreign travel has taken away some of the custom, but the town remains busy with visitors in high summer. Bingo halls, amusement arcades, ten-pin bowling and putting courses, all roughly within ten minutes' walk of the town centre, make this one of the most commercial of the Clyde resorts.

SANQUHAR
Dumfries and Galloway

On A76 27m from Dumfries.

A small market town, Sanquhar was a centre of Covenanting activity in the 1680s, when two separate declarations were posted to the mercat cross. This was at a time when episcopalianism held sway in Scotland; the Covenanters were Presbyterians trying to defend their own branch of Christianity. The first declaration, in 1680, still known as the Sanquhar Declaration, was published by Richard Cameron who, along with 60 armed associates, evaded capture for a month before being taken prisoner, and executed. James Renwick, who in 1685 published the second declaration which rejected the newly crowned James VII, suffered the same fate as Cameron in 1688. The site of the mercat cross is now marked by an obelisk. Britain's oldest post office is in the Main Street; it began business in 1763, and is still functioning today.

SEA LIFE CENTRE
Barcaldine, Strathclyde

On A828 11m N of Oban. Mar–Nov, daily. D (P) (0631 72386).

The Sea Life Centre is home to seals, conger eels and other aquatic animals, and includes some 'Touch Pools', where children can put their hands underwater and feel the different textures of the anemones, plants and rocks.

SHIPBUILDING, see panel p148.

SOLWAY FIRTH, see panel p150.

SOUTER JOHNNIE'S COTTAGE
Kirkoswald, Strathclyde

In Kirkoswald, 4m SW of Maybole. Apr–Oct, daily 1200–1700. D. NTS (065 56603/274.)

Shipbuilding

Although today **Glasgow** and the surrounding area is, in common with the rest of Britain, a service economy, up until roughly 20 years ago heavy industry predominated. Above all, it was shipbuilding that gave Glasgow its reputation as a great industrial centre, and the shipyards on the **River Clyde** that attracted hundreds of thousands of the rural poor to the city from Ireland and the Scottish Highlands. The speedy sailing ships known as clippers were used to import tea, and the tobacco trade with Virginia in the United States also caused an increase in commercial activity on the river. The real growth in shipbuilding, though, began in the early 19th century, with the coming of steam; in 1812 the *Comet* was the first sailing ship on the Clyde to use steam power as an auxiliary to its sails. By the middle of the century iron was taking over from wood as the main material used in the construction of ships, and some of the great shipping companies, such as the Cunard Line, had been founded.

The growth in defence spending throughout the 19th century and into the 20th was a huge boost to shipbuilding on the Clyde, which, by the outbreak of World War I, had become the greatest production centre in the world for the industry: it is estimated that in the years immediately before 1914, the yards on Glasgow's river were producing close to a third of the world's steamships. In the 1930s and 1940s, too, the industry was still thriving; **Clydebank**, for instance, saw the launch of the *Queen Mary* in 1934, and of Britain's last battleship, HMS *Vanguard*, ten years later. But by the 1960s, although comments of proud machismo such as 'We don't just build ships here, we build men' were still being made and ships such as the *QE2* were being launched, the industry was in decline. The Upper Clyde Shipbuilders' work-in of 1971 in many ways marked the beginning of the end for the industry; some yards survive today, but Glasgow's Finnieston Crane, once used to lift massive cargoes off the ships, now stands idle, and has taken on the status of a museum piece. Some may fondly remember the old days of the yards, while others too young to remember will romanticize the dignity of labour; but there was also the indignity of working in cramped and dangerous conditions, and, for those shipyard workers without a skilled trade, the indignity of knowing that a pittance for a wage was at least better than being unemployed.

The cottage was the home of the cobbler, or souter, John Davidson, the model for Souter Johnnie in **Robert Burn**'s poem 'Tam O' Shanter'. Stone figures of Tam, Souter Johnnie, and the landlady Nanse Tunnock – copies of the originals at the **Burns Monument** in Alloway – are in the cottage garden. Inside the cottage itself are the souter's workshop, and some of Burns's relics.

STAFFA
Strathclyde

6m NE of Iona. All year.

About half a mile by quarter of a mile, Staffa is a romantic, awe-inspiring island, its most famous spot, Fingal's Cave, having been immortalized by Mendelssohn in his *Hebrides* overture. The basaltic columns here, like the Giant's Causeway in Ireland, are so regular and orderly as to seem man-made. A number of small operators run day cruises to the island from **Mull** and **Iona**.

STIRLING
Central

Stirling's geographical position at the gateway to the Highlands has given it a central role in Scottish history. The Battle of Stirling Bridge in 1297, when the Scots under William Wallace defeated an English army, temporarily freed Scotland from the dominance of its southern neighbour. (The **Wallace Monument** stands on Abbey Craig, a mile and a half to the north-east;

the current 'Old Bridge' near the battle site dates from around 1400.) But, when King Edward I recolonized the country, the **Wars of Independence** had to be waged anew. **Stirling Castle** was, by 1314, the last significant site to remain in English hands; the Battle of **Bannockburn**, the most famous victory in Scottish history, sealed the fate of the English régime, and laid the conditions for the Declaration of Arbroath, proclaiming Scotland's independence, in 1320. In all, seven major battles have been fought in the immediate vicinity of the town.

The oldest part of Stirling, stretching steeply uphill from the centre to the castle, is well preserved and atmospheric. Argyll's Lodging, in Castle Wynd, is a fine example of an old town house, having been built in 1632 by Sir William Alexander of Menstrie, the man who founded Canada's Nova Scotia; it is now a youth hostel. The Church of the Holy Rude in St John Street is the only church in the country still in use which was the scene of a coronation, Mary Queen of Scots was crowned there in 1543 at the age of nine months, and her son James VI was proclaimed king there in 1567.

A dispute in the following century among the church's congregation led to a dividing wall being installed inside the church; the wall was removed during restoration in 1936. The church dates from the early 15th century; its tower still bears the scars of an unsuccessful cannon attack on the castle by Bonnie Prince Charlie's troops in 1746. Mar's Wark, close by at the top of Broad Street, suffered far more extensive damage during the Jacobite Rebellion, and is now but a shell of the original palace, built by the Earl of Mar in the 16th century.

The Solway Firth

With **Gretna Green** just north of the Border at the easternmost end, the coastline of the Solway Firth consists of a series of bays, wider to the west. The long, indented coastline of Dumfries and Galloway extends westwards round the estuary of the River Nith, past Southerness and **Rockcliffe**, before reaching **Kirkcudbright** Bay, **Wigtown** Bay, and finally Luce Bay. The latter is bounded on the west by the Rhinns of Galloway, which culminate in the Mull of Galloway, the southernmost tip of Scotland.

The Solway coast is rich in the history of early Christianity in these islands; **Whithorn**, about ten miles south of Wigtown, is generally agreed to be the birthplace of the religion in Scotland. St Ninian, who is thought to have been born nearby, went to Rome, was made a bishop, and returned in 397 to begin his task of converting the pagan Picts and Britons. **Isle of Whithorn** three miles to the south-east is the site of the ruined 12th-century chapel dedicated to Ninian, while St Ninian's Cave three miles to the south-west of Whithorn is thought to have been the saint's private oratory. Excavations have been going on in Whithorn for a number of years, and have unearthed the remains of Christian settlements going back to the fifth century.

The real beauty of the Solway coast is that it is still relatively unknown: even the majority of Scots who choose to holiday in their own country tend to go far further north, to **Loch Lomond**, the **Trossachs** or the Highlands. Lovers of wildlife, in particular, will find something of interest virtually every mile of the way; even the vast stretches of mud which appear when the tide is out take on a strange kind of splendour. The best area, especially for ornithology, is probably Rockcliffe. The National Trust for Scotland owns several properties in the area, including Rough Island, a 20-acre bird sanctuary.

The town's history is recounted in the Smith Art Gallery and Museum in Dumbarton Road, which also puts on exhibitions of contemporary art. Just off Dumbarton Road is the King's Park, once the hunting grounds for the court when they stayed in Stirling; it is now a public park, although houses have encroached on the original area. Now grassed over, the King's Knot opposite the park was an octagonal mound, part of the formal gardens laid out beneath the castle. Even in the more modern areas of Stirling, evidence of the Middle Ages and Renaissance is never far away. The Thistle Centre, an anonymous shopping mall of the type to be found in any British city, can at least boast the Bastion, the remains of a circular defence tower which was part of the 16th-century town wall. The wall is the best surviving example in Scotland; one of the most pleasant and informative walks in the town is around the wall, from Dumbarton Road to the castle, and thence back down to the old town.

A mile east of the town centre, off Riverside Drive, lies Cambuskenneth Abbey, founded by King David I for the Augustinian order in 1147. Robert the Bruce's parliament met there in 1326; James III and his queen are buried in the grounds. Although much of the stone was taken away after the Reformation, the restored Bell Tower, originally built in 1300, still stands.

STIRLING CASTLE
Stirling, Central

Apr–Sept, Mon–Sat 0930–1715, Sun 1030–1645; Oct–Mar, Mon–Sat 0930–1630, Sun 1230–1545. D (P). HS (031–244 3101).

Just why Stirling and its castle held such strategic importance in the Middle Ages, to the extent that the battle for control of the castle (**Bannockburn**, 1314) determined the fate of Scotland, is immediately evident when gazing from the castle battlements. Built on a 250-foot-high rock, it commands the Lowlands spread out below it to east, west and south, and guards the Highlands to the north; holding the castle meant effective control of Stirling Bridge, then the main crossing-point of the River Forth. The panoramic view from the castle must be one of the best, and most extensive, in Scotland: from Bannockburn just a couple of miles to the south, to Ben Lomond far off in the west, to the Ochil Hills to the north, and to the Pentlands to the south. It is probable that the castle hill was first fortified in the Iron Age, and certain that the first castle in historical times was timber-built; the current building dates largely from the 15th and 16th centuries, although the original stone construction was in the 12th century. Walking up Castle Hill today, the first building on the esplanade is the visitor centre, managed by the National Trust for Scotland; it includes a shop, and an audio-visual display on the castle. In the castle itself can be seen the Stirling Heads, some of the original collection of wooden medallions which covered the ceiling of the King's Own Hall (later known as the King's Presence Chamber). The Douglas Garden is said to be where the body of William, 8th Earl of Douglas, was thrown after being killed during a quarrel with King James II in 1452, part of a quarrel between the Stewarts and Douglases only resolved in favour of the monarch's family with the capture three years

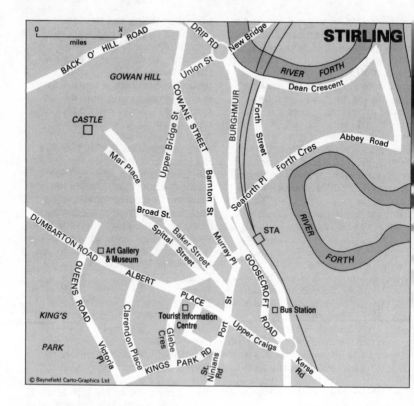

Town plan of Stirling

later of **Threave Castle**. Despite that gruesome episode, the garden is one of the most pleasant and evocative parts of the castle.

STIRLING UNIVERSITY
Bridge of Allan, Central

On A9 2m N of Stirling.

Opened as part of the expansion of higher education in the 1960s, Stirling University has a unique two-term (semester) system. The campus is splendidly scenic, the student residences being separated from the teaching and administrative centres by a man-made loch, which is spanned by a bridge. The university's MacRobert Arts Centre, which includes a gallery and a threatre-cum-cinema, is open to the public. The 19th-century Airthrey Castle, used as a maternity hospital earlier this century, now houses the student radio station, and is also used for teaching.

STRANRAER
Dumfries and Galloway

Off A75 10m W of Glenluce.

The ferry for Larne, in Northern Ireland, leaves from Stranraer, making it principally a transit town. It is, however, a sheltered spot – which is why the ferry was moved from **Portpatrick** – and, although not itself the most picturesque of places, offers good facilities for holidaymakers, particularly those who enjoy fishing or boating. Stranraer Museum, in the Old Town Hall in George Street, is chiefly a local history museum.

STRATHCLYDE COUNTRY PARK
Strathhaven, Strathclyde

Off M74 between Hamilton and Bothwell interchanges. All year. Tours: Easter–Sept, daily at 1500, also July–Aug; Sat and Sun at 1900; winter, Sat and Sun only at 1400. D. Free (0698 66155).

The park offers a number of nature trails, and a good range of sporting facilities, including boating on the man-made loch. Hamilton Mausoleum in the park, built as a chapel and crypt for the Dukes of Hamilton, is reputed to have the longest echo of any building in Europe.

SWEETHEART ABBEY
Dumfries and Galloway

At New Abbey, on A710, 7½m S of Dumfries. Apr–Sept, Mon–Sat 0930–1900; Sun 1400–1900; Oct–Mar, Mon–Sat 0930–1600, Sun 1400–1600. D (P). HS (031–244 3101).

Devorgilla Balliol, mother of King John Balliol, founded the abbey in 1273 in memory of her husband, also John. The name derives from her having carried her husband's embalmed heart with her; after her death, the heart was buried with her in front of the altar. Although a ruin, the magificent building still dominates **New Abbey**.

TARBERT
Strathclyde

On A83 on W shore of Loch Fyne.

Once one of the most important
herring ports in the area,
picturesque Tarbert is now a quieter
place, more used to visits from
tourists than from fishing boats.
Just north of the town is Stonefield
Castle, built by Sir William Playfair
in 1838. Overlooking Loch Fyne,
it is set in 50 acres of attractive
woodland.

THREAVE CASTLE
Dumfries and Galloway

*N of A75 3m W of Castle Douglas.
Apr–Sept, Mon–Sat 0930–1900, Sun
1400–1900; Oct–Mar, Mon–Sat 0930–1600,
Sun 1400–1600. HS (031-244 3101).*

Built in the 14th century by
Archibald the Grim, Lord of
Galloway, Threave Castle stands on
a small island in the River Dee, to
reach which you must ring a bell
and wait for the custodian to row
out and take you back. Threave
was the last stronghold to capitulate
to King James II during his bitter
dispute with the Douglas family.

THREAVE GARDENS AND WILDFOWL REFUGE
Dumfries and Galloway

*Off A75 1m W of Castle Douglas. Gardens:
all year, daily 0900–sunset. Wildfowl refuge:
Nov–Mar. D (P). NTS (0556 2575).*

The garden specializes in daffodils,
nearly 200 varieties of which bloom
every spring. The Victorian house,

which is closed to the public, is the
National Trust for Scotland's School
of Horticulture. The wildfowl refuge
nearby is a roosting and feeding
place on the River Dee for many
species of wild geese and duck.

TIBETAN MONASTERY, see KAGYU SAMYE LING.

TILLICOULTRY
Central

On A91 10m NE of Stirling.

One of the attractive Hillfoots
villages, Tillicoultry, at the foot
of Mill Glen, was once a thriving
centre of the woollen mill industry;
the Clock Mill Heritage Centre in
Upper Mill Street contains displays
about the heyday of the industry,
and sells local knitwear. Another
disused mill is now the site of
what is now the best-known thing
about the village – Sterling, Britain's
largest furniture store, so familiar
through its TV advertising that some
residents of Tillicoultry now borrow
its slogan and ironically claim to
come from 'The Big One'.

TIREE, ISLE OF
Strathclyde

7m W of Mull.

Almost identical in size to its
neighbour **Coll**, Tiree is a low, flat
island, with only two hills above
400 feet. It usually has more hours
of sunshine than anywhere else
in Scotland, but is also extremely
windy: this combination of

The Trossachs

O riginally the name only of the wooded glen between Loch Katrine and Loch Achray, the Trossachs today is generally taken to refer to a much wider area, its rough boundaries stretching from **Callander** in the east to Queen Elizabeth National Forest Park in the west – although that reaches virtually to the shores of Loch Lomond. In common with the loch, the Trossachs straddle the Highland Boundary Fault, which accounts for the diversity of scenery within the area, one of the most picturesque in the country. The David Marshall Lodge near **Aberfoyle** provides information on walks and drives within the area, as does the Forest Information Centre in Strathyre. Aberfoyle stands just below the steep slopes which mark the southern edge of the Highlands; from the top of Duke's Pass the view is of the Lowlands laid out flat beneath. Callander includes the Rob Roy and Trossachs Visitor Centre, while **Rob Roy Macgregor** himself lived and died in **Balquhidder** at the eastern end of Loch Voil. A short distance north-west of Balquhidder is **Lochearnhead**, and its popular watersports centre; to the north of Balquhidder lie the lands of **Breadalbane**. Again like Loch Lomond, the Trossachs owe much of their popularity to the ease with which they can be reached from the Lowland cities and towns; this can make parts of the area seem overcrowded, at least in high summer, to those who prefer a peaceful, undisturbed day's walking. The Trossachs are in fact best explored on foot, and, in spring and autumn, the scenery has a much wilder look to it. The area has abundant wildlife, including red deer, mink, foxes and ptarmigans, as well as two specially protected species, the golden eagle and the peregrine falcon.

conditions explains why it has latterly become an extremely popular spot with windsurfers. Cattle- and sheep-farming are the main occupations of the islanders. Although the sandy beaches are excellent and the number of tourists is increasing, Tiree is still relatively peaceful in summer.

TONGLAND POWER STATION
Dumfries and Galloway

By A711 2m N of Kirkcudbright. May–Aug, tours Mon–Sat 1000, 1130, 1400, 1530. Free (0557 30114/0294 822311).

Scottish Power, who own this hydro-electric power station and dam, lay on free transport from **Kirkcudbright** for anyone wishing to go on the guided tour. A video and displays tell more about the workings of the station.

TORHOUSE STONE CIRCLE
Dumfries and Galloway

Off B733, 4m W of Wigtown. All year. Free. HS (031–244 3101).

Believed to date from the Bronze Age, this is a circle of 19 boulders, standing on the edge of a low mound, in the middle of which are three more boulders. The site was probably of astronomical and/or religious significance.

TROON
Strathclyde

On B749 5m S of Irvine.

One of Ayrshire's many renowned golfing venues, Troon is a small, attractive coastal holiday town, standing on an outcrop of land. The Postage Stamp at Royal Troon is one of the best-known holes in golf.

TROSSACHS, see panel p155.

TURNBERRY
Strathclyde

On A77 6m N of Girvan.

Turnberry Castle, of which little now remains, is said to be the birthplace of Robert the Bruce, although the same claim is made for **Lochmaben**. Certainly it was a stronghold of the Bruce family. Originally part of the Marquis of Ailsa's Culzean estate, Turnberry golf course was established as a leading venue for the sport by the turn of the century. Taken over for military use in World War II, it was reclaimed afterwards, and a new course built.

VENNIEHILL
Dumfries and Galloway

Off A75 in Gatehouse of Fleet. All year.
Free. NTS.

Venniehill is a 3½-acre field at
the west end of the town's main
street, with a viewpoint at the top of
the hill.

WALLACE MONUMENT
near Stirling, Central

Off A997 (Hillfoots Road), 1½m NE
of Stirling. June–Aug, daily 1000–1800;
Apr–May, Sept, daily 1000–1700; Feb–Mar,
Oct, Mon–Tues, Fri–Sun 1000–1600. D (P)
(0786 72140).

Standing up on the 300-foot high
Abbey Craig, the monument, which
is itself 220 feet high, commemorates
Sir William Wallace, the victor of
the Battle of **Stirling** Bridge, and the
initiator of the **Wars of Independence**
against England. Completed in
1869, the tower houses the Wallace
sword, used by Sir William, the
Hall of Arms, a collection of
mainly medieval weapons, and
the Hall of Heroes, a number of
busts of famous Scots, among them
Robert the Bruce, **Robert Burns** and
John Knox, and one of Gladstone,
who, although born in Liverpool,
presumably qualified by virtue of
being Prime Minister at the time
the monument was opened. A
statue of Wallace stands on the
side of the tower. Two audio-visual
programmes may be viewed in the
Sword Room: one tells of the life
and times of Wallace, while the
other is a guide to the flora, fauna
and history of the Forth valley.

WANLOCKHEAD
Dumfries and Galloway

On B797 1m S of Leadhills.

Just about the northernmost centre
of population in Dumfries and
Galloway, Wanlockhead claims to
be the highest village in Scotland, at
1380 feet just above its Strathclyde
neighbour, Leadhills. The Museum
of Scottish Lead Mining in the
village includes cottages furnished
in the style of 1740 and 1890, an
indoor museum with relics of the
industry, and an outdoor museum
with sections of the old mine
preserved.

WARS OF INDEPENDENCE,
see panel p158.

WEAVER'S COTTAGE
Kilbarchan, Strathclyde

Shuttle Street, Kilbarchan, off A737 12m
SW of Glasgow. Jun–Aug, daily 1400–1700;
Apr–May, Sept–Oct, Tue, Thur, Sat–Sun
1400–1700. D (P). NTS (050 57 5588).

The cottage typifies the dwelling of
an 18th-century handloom-weaver,
and contains weaving equipment of
the period.

WEST HIGHLAND WAY, see
panel p159.

WHITHORN, ISLE OF
Dumfries and Galloway

3m SE of Whithorn.

The Wars of Independence

When Margaret, the Maid of Norway, died in 1290, it was the signal for King Edward I of England to attempt to subjugate his northern neighbour. The young Scottish queen had been betrothed to the Prince of Wales, and it has been argued that, had she lived, Scotland and England would have come to a harmonious union. Edward, invited to adjudicate, ruled that the Scottish crown should go not to Robert the Bruce, but to John Balliol who, after some resistance, surrendered his kingdom to the English. The first wave of resistance was led by Sir William Wallace, who embarked on a military campaign against the occupying army, and scored a notable victory at the Battle of **Stirling** Bridge in 1297. Betrayed to the English, Wallace was hung, drawn and quartered in London, in 1305. He remains one of Scotland's two great national heroes, and is commemorated by the **Wallace Monument**.

The other hero, Robert the Bruce, was declared king the year after Wallace's death. At first a fugitive in a seemingly hopeless condition, he fought an astute guerrilla campaign, ambushing the English forces when least expected, and driving them out of Scotland's castles. The Battle of **Bannockburn** in 1314 was the triumphant conclusion of Bruce's struggle, and arguably the most important event in Scotland's history. Taking on a numerically superior force which had been sent to relieve the beleaguered English garrison at **Stirling Castle**, the Scots routed their opponents, thus regaining the last castle to have been held by the invaders. Six years later, the Declaration of Arbroath formally announced Scotland's independence. 'For as long as one hundred of us shall remain alive,' it stated, 'we shall never consent to submit to the rule of the English.'

The West Highland Way

Ninety-five miles long, the West Highland Way runs from **Milngavie**, on the outskirts of **Glasgow**, to Fort William. In that relatively short distance the surroundings move from one extreme of Scotland to another – from the heartland of urban Strathclyde to the remoteness of Ben Nevis. The Way itself follows a variety of paths, from ancient drove roads to disused railway lines. Because the terrain is rougher in some northern sections of the Way, walkers who plan to go the distance are strongly recommended to proceed from south to north, thus allowing themselves time to 'acclimatize' on the easier section. From Milngavie the Way goes first to Drymen, once a useful source of protection money for **Rob Roy Macgregor**, and then on to Balmaha, almost in the south-eastern corner of **Loch Lomond**. From Balmaha it is a seven-mile hike to **Rowardennan**, then another six to Inversnaid, and then the same distance to Inverarnan at the northern end of the Loch. Almost all the distances between the recognized staging posts are of this order: another six miles from Inverarnan is **Crianlarich**, from where Tyndrum is a further seven. Only at the northern end, once the Way is in Highland Region, do the distances between stops grow, and the country becomes more open and arduous.

Adequate clothing is a must, as is the ability to use a map and compass. The West Highland Way is an excellent introduction to Scotland's contrasting scenery for everyone from family groups and Sunday strollers to hardened hill-walkers. The regular stops along most of the route allow the inexperienced or more leisurely walker to progress slowly northwards, taking anything up to a fortnight to reach Fort William, allowing perhaps for the odd diversion to explore Loch Lomond or relax in **Crianlarich**. A full guide and map to the West Highland Way, published by HMSO, is available from most bookshops.

No longer an island, Isle of Whithorn is a picturesque fishing village. Most of the fishermen's cottages are now used by holidaymakers. The village contains the ruined St Ninian's Chapel, which dates from the 13th century. Two miles west, on the shore by Kilsdale, St Ninian's Cave contains early Christian carvings.

WHITHORN DIG AND VISITOR CENTRE
Whithorn, Dumfries and Galloway

45–47 George Street, Whithorn, 10m S of Wigtown. Easter–Oct, daily 1030–1700, Sun 1300–1700. D (P) (09885 508).

Scotland's first known Christian community, founded by St Ninian in 397, is now the site of a major archaeological dig. Visitors can watch the dig in progress, and see some of the finds unearthed to date, which include remnants of the early Christian buildings, medieval graves, and a variety of fragments which have advanced the understanding of the way of life of Dark Ages and medieval Scots.

WHITHORN PRIORY AND MUSEUM
Whithorn, Dumfries and Galloway

Main Street, Whithorn, 10m S of Wigtown. Apr–Sept, Mon–Sat 0930–1900, Sun 1400–1900; Oct–Mar, Sat 0930–1600, Sun 1400–1600. D (P). HS (031–244 3101).

Alongside the ruins of the 12th-century priory stands the museum, which contains some early Christian crosses; others are still visible, carved into the rock of the priory itself.

WIGTOWN
Dumfries and Galloway

On A714 7m S of Newton Stewart.

Now a peaceful resort on the western shore of Wigtown Bay, this was the site of one of the most notorious episodes in the 17th-century struggle between the Presbyterian Covenanters and the government. In 1685 two women, having been found guilty of attending Covenanters' meetings, were tied to stakes on the shore and drowned by the rising tide. The graves of both are in Wigtown churchyard; a pillar on the shore and a monument on the hill also stand in remembrance.